5-DAY JUICE CHALLENGE

5-DAY JUICE CHALLENGE

THE JUICE
DETOX DIET

**JUICE MASTER
JASON VALE**
★★★★★

Thorsons

Other books by Jason Vale:

The Juice Master's Slim for Life
The Juice Master's Ultimate Fast Food
Chocolate Busters: The Easy Way to Kick It
The Juice Master – Turbo-charge Your Life in 14 Days
The Juice Master: Keeping It Simple
The Juice Master: Juice Yourself Slim
The Juice Master Diet: 7lbs in 7 Days
The Funky Fresh Juice Book
Kick the Drink … Easily!
Super Juice Me! 28-Day Juice Diet
5:2 Juice Diet

When it comes to juicing for health and well-being there's only one man for the job, the undisputed king of juicing Jason Vale! He will literally change your life!

Alesha Dixon

The contents of this book should be used as a general guideline only.
Nothing in this book should be taken as medical advice or diagnosis, and
you should always consult with a qualified medical practitioner before
starting on any weight-loss programme, or if you have any concerns about
your health. The author and the publishers do not accept any responsibility
for any loss or harm that may occur from your use or misuse of this book or
your failure to seek appropriate medical advice.

In rare circumstances some juices can interfere with certain medication.
If you are taking any medication please make absolutely sure it is not
affected by freshly extracted juices.

Thorsons
An imprint of HarperCollins*Publishers*
1 London Bridge Street
London SE1 9GF

www.harpercollins.co.uk

First published as *5lbs in 5 Days* by HarperThorsons 2014

This updated Thorsons edition published by arrangement with
Retro Juicer 2016

1 3 5 7 9 10 8 6 4 2

A catalogue record of this book is available from the British Library

ISBN 978-0-00-821954-3

Printed and bound in Great Britain by Clays Ltd, St Ives plc

MIX
Paper from
responsible sources
FSC™ C007454

CONTENTS

Part 4: The Rough After Plan

FOREWORD

Dr Justine Dawkins

I am a full-time general practitioner (family doctor) from Bridgend in South Wales, UK. I am 43, a wife and mother of three, and the only child of a PE teacher and a welder. I was fortunate that my mum was into healthy eating even in the 1970s when it didn't really exist. We didn't own a chip pan or a deep fat fryer. Mum knew fizzy drinks were bad for us, so when the Corona Van came round the houses once a week the man knew not to bother knocking on our door. I had a better than average start in life, I think. That didn't stop me eating my fair share of fast food and takeaways as a student, not to mention the hundreds of chicken-and mushroom-flavoured Pot Noodles I must have consumed over a five-year medical course. (I have done five London Marathons since then to make up for it.) I have been practising medicine for over 20 years. During this time I have seen the population of my country expand, literally. Hand in hand with the obesity epidemic come inevitable illnesses such as type 2 diabetes, high cholesterol, raised blood pressure, heart disease, stroke, arthritis and chronic pain, and other difficulties including low self-esteem, depression and relationship breakdown – the list goes on.

Often now, it is slim people who turn heads, not just because they may be more attractive to the eye, but because we're all gradually getting fatter. I find myself wondering how these people manage to stay slim. Some are lucky enough to have personal trainers or the time to spend hours in the gym. A few are lucky enough to have inherited good skinny genes (pardon the pun).

Or perhaps they have discovered Jason Vale?

I hope Jason will forgive me for referring to him as a discovery, but, as most memorable discoveries are usually found by accident, I think it applies.

Jason's books are easy to read, but like any good author they leave you wanting more. As soon as I finished the aforementioned pink book I strayed back to Amazon to look at his other publications. *7lbs in 7 Days* immediately caught my eye, as it would for anyone who (like me) had 7lbs or more to lose. My next dilemma was how to not regain the half stone that I had just so easily and enjoyably lost. Never fear, *Turbo-charge Your Life in 14 Days* was next, followed by *Slim for Life* to consolidate everything. That was my journey to becoming fitter, healthier and slimmer. Since then I continue to re-read bits of the books and I have recommended all of Jason's titles to many of my patients.

The juicing community is growing in an exponential manner, evidenced by the UK-wide shortage of juicers this summer. My neighbours are juicing (and shrinking). My friends ask me: 'are you still juicing?' It's a weird thing to ask; of course I am, juice is my fix. I can't leave it alone and I was desperate to read this new book of Jason's and try out the new 5-day programme!

I have so much more I could say about Jason Vale, Juicy Oasis and the amazing, life-changing results I have witnessed first-hand, but my remit was to write a foreword, not a book. I don't look at this as an endorsement of Jason Vale's ideas – I personally subscribe to them out of choice and I have given you a snippet of my journey.

You all have a choice. I hope you chose what is right for you.

Dr Justine Dawkins, GP

The Weight Just Falls Off!

After dropping **9 pounds in 5 days** I know to incorporate a juice a day to get more than my 5 a day!

> *Bronagh Waugh*
> *(actress on* Hollyoaks*)*

I've lost **10 lbs** ...

> *Esterina*

9lb lost in 5 days! I found it easier to do than 7lbs in 7 days

> *Katie*

Down 7.5lbs after 5in5!

> *Jo*

Day 5 (of 5lbs in 5 days) and **I've lost a whopping 7lbs**

> *Natalie*

Hubby and I completed 5lbs in 5 days this week and **lost 29lbs between us!**

> *Rachael*

Let's cut
TO THE
JUICY
CHASE!

I

If you are reading this book, the chances are that unless you have picked it up for research, you are looking to improve your health in some way. Given the title, it is probably also safe to say that you wouldn't mind dropping a few pounds ... or maybe five, maybe even ten. And also that you'd like to drop that excess weight in super-fast time. Chances are you are looking for a programme that can achieve rapid weight loss, while at the same time providing a follow-on system to make sure you keep the weight off for good. If this is you, then, as corny as it sounds, you've picked up the right book.

I have been writing about juicing for weight loss and optimum health for the past 15 years and everything I have done up until now has lead me to this – the most effective *rapid healthy* weight-loss 'juice detox' to date. This is not an easy feat, due to the incredible success of this book's predecessor.

THE 7LBS IN 7 DAYS PHENOMENON

My previous book, *7lbs in 7 Days: Super Juice Diet*, was released in 2006 and went straight to number 1 of *all* books on Amazon, not simply in its category, but of every other book available. On play.com it even knocked *The Da Vinci Code* from the number 1 slot (which, as you can imagine, is not something I mention very often ... well, you know). Even as I write this page, the app is number 1 in 'food and drink' on iTunes (Jamie Oliver is number 2) and the book is number 1 in its category on Amazon (it's been there for eight years). It has gone on to sell well over a million copies and has been translated into many other languages.

Many celebrities were reported to have done the 7-Day Juice Master Diet, including Katie Price, Sarah Jessica Parker, Drew Barrymore, Jennifer Aniston, Alesha Dixon, Samantha Womack, Sarah Harding, Linda Barker, Kerry Katona, Natasha Hamilton, Beverley Knight and Scott Mills ... the list goes on and on. I'm not entirely sure if all the celebs that have been reported to have done the plan actually did, but it gives you a sense of the kind of buzz the book created.

What the 7-day *juice only* plan showed above all else was just how much the body will naturally heal if given the right tools and the right environment to do so. It is safe to say that I've seen just about every common lifestyle disease either improve, or be completely eradicated, with the use of *freshly extracted* juice and a very well-thought-through plan. What was even more incredible was to see these common health conditions improve so dramatically and so quickly. In the space of just seven days on the *fresh juice only* programme, some lifelong health issues disappeared completely.

FAT 'N' FLAKY BOY!

I have not only been spreading the 'juice revolution' for years, I have been on the journey myself. I have worn the fat and unhealthy T-shirt. I used to be 15 stone 2lb (96kg) (I'm only 5ft 7.1in) and was covered from head to toe in a severe skin condition called psoriasis; I had bad asthma (using the asthma pump up to 14 times a day), extremely bad hay fever (to the point where I couldn't function) and larger breasts than the average woman (not a good look for a dude). I also used to smoke between two and three packets of cigarettes a day and was a heavy alcohol drinker.

I cut out the rubbish, started to juice and the weight just fell off – *effortlessly*. My asthma vanished and my skin completely cleared up. This is what inspired me to want to start the Juice Revolution and 'Juice the World', a mission I am still focusing on today. I also stopped smoking and, as I write this, at 44 years of age, I can honestly say I feel better today than I did when I was 24. Nothing comes close to the *healthy* but extremely *rapid* weight-loss ability of a well-thought-through juicing programme. When I say I have seen it all, I mean I have seen it all.

ONE DISEASE – ONE SOLUTION

I have seen cholesterol levels drop from 8 points to 5 in that short time with no drug therapy whatsoever. I have seen asthma improve to the extent where people have not only reduced their medication, but stopped using it altogether ...

in just seven days. I have even seen someone at my retreat with type 1 diabetes reduce their medication by 75 per cent within just the first five days of juicing. I have seen IBS, arthritis, eczema, Crohn's, endometriosis, high blood pressure, type 2 diabetes and even ulcerative colitis symptoms completely vanish with a juicing programme.

I have seen skin glow and energy levels go through the roof, cravings for junk disappear and, of course, and what for some will be the most important aspect, some utterly ridiculous weight-loss results – and I do mean ridiculous.

I received one email where a guy dropped 19lbs in a week – in one week! (I'll share that later in this book). I got a message from Lord Harris of London no less (it's not every day you get a mail from a Lord); he'd read the book and dropped 42lbs in just three months; his cholesterol also went from the 'danger of getting heart disease' zone to 'perfect'. One person dropped over 200lbs by introducing fresh juice into their lives. Another read the book and within three months of juicing her endometriosis, which she had suffered from for eight years and which had been a factor in several miscarriages, vanished! She had tried all kinds of drugs for many years and nothing helped.

I saw my own health be completely transformed because of fresh juicing too. The average drop was 7lbs for women and 10lbs for men. The vast majority of these people not only kept the initial weight off, but went on to achieve their ideal body weight because juicing became a way of life.

Whether it's from the emails or videos people have sent in, from hearing first-hand accounts on my health retreats, or in my own life, I have seen some miraculous changes in both health and weight loss which happen in a *very* short space of time.

CONDENSE SUCCESS

Turn Years into Months
Months into Weeks
Weeks into Days

And if we cut to the chase, isn't that what we are all looking for? A simple, *highly effective*, healthy, but moreover, *rapid* way to drop weight so we can get lean, be thin, wear what the hell we want and feel amazing? We want our skin to glow, our hair to shine and our stomach to be flat! We want to turn years into months, months into weeks and weeks into days – don't we? We don't want to lose weight 'gradually' and to 'be patient' – we want results and we want them yesterday! This is why I am always looking to condense success, as I say. As in, I am always looking for a way to achieve the same level of success in a shorter period of time. I also constantly look for ways to make that success even easier and more enjoyable. This is precisely what I have done with *5-Day Juice Challenge: The Juice Detox Diet*.

If there were any challenges with the *7lbs in 7 days: Super Juice Diet*, it was the fact it was over a seven-day period and included the weekend. Weekends tend to be an extremely precious time for many people and the last thing many wanted to do was to miss out on meals or evenings out with friends and family. I wanted to develop a powerful juice *and* unique fitness programme that gave the same level of success, but in just five days; I wanted to give people their weekends back. I also wanted to develop a simple follow-on plan which would enable people to reach their ultimate dream health and weight and keep it off. *5-Day Juice Challenge: The Juice Detox Diet* does exactly that. People who have followed it to the letter drop an average of 7lbs, the same as the seven-day plan; many people who have done the programme have lost an incredible 10lbs *in five days*. Dramatic losses such as this will only happen if you follow the five-day juice and Super After-burn exercise programme to the letter.

But It's Not Healthy to Lose More than 2lbs a Week ... Blah, Blah, Blah!

I will cover this later in the book, but it needs addressing now as well, for whenever I mention such dramatic weight losses in such short periods of time, many people start with the predictable mantra that 'it's not healthy to lose so much so quickly'. In fact, the number of people I hear saying that 'it's not healthy to lose more than 2lbs a week' is a joke. You might know some of them; you may even be one of them if you are reading this for research, but did you know there is no scientific evidence *whatsoever* to show that it's unhealthy to lose more than 2lbs a week?

It's like the 'you must drink 2 litres of water a day' mantra – it's a myth that has been perpetuated for years, but which no one has challenged or questioned. There is an old saying that if you tell a lie long enough, strong enough and hard enough, then even the person who started the lie ends up believing it. This has been the case with this utter nonsense about it being unhealthy, and some doctors and medics would even go as far as to say dangerous, to lose more than 2lbs a week. Nope, not joking, they use the word 'dangerous'!

Now going to fight in a war-torn part of the world for your country is dangerous, or putting your head in a hot oven, but drinking the juice contained within vegetables that is specifically designed to feed every cell of the human body is clearly not. I say clearly not, but we are in a world where some highly intelligent doctors and 'experts' cannot see this clearly and continue to preach the 'don't lose more than 2lb a week' mantra because they believe it to be 'dangerous'.

As I said, I will cover this later in the book but for now all you need to know is if you hear anyone saying that living on freshly extracted juice for five days and dropping 5–10lbs in that short space of time is dangerous, please know it's total and utter nonsense.

This Programme Works
100 Per Cent of the Time
For 100 Per Cent of the People

All you actually need to know is that if you have excess weight to lose, it works. Not only does it work but it works 100 per cent of the time for 100 per cent of the people. I know this because it's been tried and tested over and over again and, as mentioned, this five-day plan – *if done to the letter* – can be just as effective as the seven-day one. All you have to do is follow these three simple instructions. If you do, success is yours every single time.

1. READ THE BOOK

Before you start the programme you need to read the whole book, *with the exception of:*

★ 'The Rough After Plan' (pp. 191–197);
★ 'The Low-H.I. Way of Life' (pp. 199–209);
★ 'The Law of Four' (pp. 211–216); and
★ 'Be Limitless and Make Your Life Extraordinary' (pp. 217–226).

You need to read everything else. This includes the Q & A section (pp. 239–254).

2. FOLLOW THE VERY SIMPLE PROGRAMME ... *TO THE LETTER!*

This programme has been carefully thought through in terms of both nutrition and effectiveness; please do not veer away from it. If you want the results it has to offer, follow the exact recipe laid out and you will get the same results as everyone else.

3. ON DAY 5 READ THE REST ...

On day 5 read the following chapters:

★ 'The Rough After Plan' (pp. 191–197); 'The Low-H.I. Way of Life' (pp. 199–209); 'The Law of Four' (pp. 211–216); and 'Be Limitless and Make Your Life Extraordinary' (pp. 217–226).

Make a note of this now!

You are welcome to read these chapters before you start the programme, but you need to re-read them on Day 5 too. What you need to do after the five days is just as important as the five days themselves, so do not miss this instruction. Those chapters will make more sense to you on Day 5 as you'll feel very differently by then, both mentally and physically. This is because any withdrawal from refined sugars, fats and caffeine, would have subsided, leaving you free to really take on board the after plan.

THAT'S IT AND THAT'S ALL!

Follow these three simple instructions and in just five days you will feel a way, I'd lay money on, you haven't done in years. Yes, you'll lose weight – 5lbs and then some, more like 7lbs to be fair and for some 10lbs – but it's how your mind is going to feel that will surprise you most. The most common feedback I get is people saying they had no idea just how much weight would also be lifted from their mind. What many refer to as 'Brain Fog' or 'Fussy Thinking' seems to completely lift; people say they are just sharper. When the blood that circulates through your brain is loaded with the vital key nutrients required to feed the cells, and it's not dealing with refined sugars, fats, alcohol and other rubbish, your head becomes clear and you start being totally on top of your game. Do not underestimate what can be achieved when you feel both mentally and physically fired up. Every single aspect of your life changes for the better.

My ultimate aim for this book is not for you to simply juice yourself up for five days, drop some weight and feel good for the party. No. My aim is for you to see, but more importantly, feel such a difference in yourself that you are compelled to adopt a juicy fitness lifestyle for life. Yes the title is *5-Day Juice Challenge* but I am hoping that's a sprat to catch a mackerel. In other words, I am hoping it doesn't just lure you in, but catches you fully. For most people there's often much bigger fish to fry than a quick 5lbs and, if you are like most people, you will be so recharged at the end of five days that this will act as a catalyst to much bigger changes on the weight loss and health front. So you may well feel you'll be doing it simply to fit into that little black dress (or skinny jeans) but, chances are, you'll never grow out of them again.

READ THE BOOK!

I don't know much about anything else, but I do know juicing and I do know the importance of the right frame of mind. Because of this, and in order for this programme to be easy, I have advised you to read the book first. Please do not skip ahead and just start. You need the right mental preparation or the chances are you will fail. The reason I believe *7lbs in*

7 Days has been so successful, and my theory is backed up by tens of thousands of testimonials, is because of the first instruction: read the book.

As I'm sure you know, the vast majority of books of this nature never actually get read. In the UK, we buy more recipe books than any other European country, yet at the same time we buy twice as many takeaways. We are very good at buying books, but reading them and, moreover, acting on them, is an entirely different matter.

I do know that my style of writing isn't for everyone. I often say I write books but I am in no way an author in the true sense of the word. I am not here to win any literary awards, but simply to do one thing and one thing alone: provide you with relevant information which I hope will inspire you to *want* to do the programme in order to experience the results it has to offer. Once you experience those results it will inspire you to *want* to eat well and move your body on a daily basis and thus create lifelong change. The key is to get you to do the programme in the first place and I will use capitals, over-use exclamation marks and repeat the same points over and over again to make sure this is a book you will act upon! (There you see, an instant overuse of an exclamation mark, proving I am a man of my word.)

We live in a super-fast world and the temptation to skip the reading and just get on with the programme is a strong one. The challenge with that is you can start unprepared and fall at the first fence. The one advantage of the way I write is you will fly through this book in no time at all. (One of the most frustrating things about writing books is just how stupidly quickly they are read in comparison to how long they take to write!) You will find that you'll rattle through this book in no time at all. It will take less than one day to read the whole book (for some just a couple of hours) and it makes a huge difference when you do. It is the difference between starting fully prepared and going in blind. I have only given three instructions; adhere to all of them and you'll not only *get through* it, you'll enjoy the process too.

PUT ME IN YOUR POCKET!

For those who feel they need or want a little extra help, I also have a 5lbs in 5 Days app, which can be a very useful additional tool. For the cynics out there, I am more than aware that seems like an advert, but the full programme is all here in this book (the app is completely optional and you don't *need* it to complete the programme). I'm simply mentioning it at the start because many people have told me it made the difference between total success and a fridge full of mouldy fruit and veg!

This is what I love about technology; you have instant access to videos on your smartphone, tablet or phablet, meaning you effectively have a coach in your pocket in times of need. The app also has an intro video, five full coaching videos (one for each day), ten recipe videos and a final video explaining exactly what to do after the plan so you don't undo all of your good work. Once again, you have *everything* you need in this book, but the app may help for those who like a bit of coaching each day as well as visually seeing how to make all the recipes.

For some people I know this will be a simple 'drop a few pounds before the party' thing, but having done this for years, I am more than aware that for many this is hopefully the final thing that will kick-start them to the land of the slim, trim and healthy. This is why I make no apologies for suggesting the app as a tool to help. Anything that helps anyone to actually complete this programme in order to move them from where they are to where they want, or often, need to be on the health front, is worth mentioning.

PEOPLE POWER!

I have been doing whatever I can to convince people of the incredible health and weight-loss powers of freshly extracted juice for over a decade now, but no matter what scientific evidence I present or nutritional facts about the unique juice contained within the fibres of fruits and vegetables, nothing – and I do mean nothing – inspires people to jump on the juicing lifestyle more than others who have been there and got the truly remarkable results. Nothing motivates more than hearing of someone who, in such a short space of time, has lost huge amounts of weight or had significant changes to their mental and physical health. Nothing also inspires more to start a programme of this nature than hearing stories of people who not only lost a significant amount of weight in super-fast time, but also went on to reach their ideal weight and kept that weight off.

The stories you are about to read are one hundred per cent genuine and unsolicited; not one has been doctored or exaggerated in anyway. When looking for letters and emails to give as examples of the successes people have on this programme, it was almost impossible to choose. I have *thousands* to choose from! Some of you may be aware that I released a taster version of the e-book in March 2013. It was available for just one week coinciding with our annual Global Juice Detox and resulted in thousands of downloads, and thousands of emails, Facebook messages and testimonials, a few of which you will see here.

I have just spent the last few hours reading through them, and I'm now questioning why I am writing the rest of the book. There are two points to the first part of the book:

1 to get you inspired; and
2 to make you realize just how easy it can be.

We'll get to the making it easy part later. Once you start to read the following testimonials you will be champing at the bit to get started. Please, please make a point of reading the stories, and also my comments below them, as the combination dispels many of the common myths about juicing. If you have tried any of my juice programmes before then I doubt the following stories will actually come as a surprise, but if this is your first outing into my juicy world, then ...

Prepare

TO BE

INSPIRED

2

OMGoodness! **I've lost 11 pounds ... YES, 11 pounds!**
I feel awesome. My blood sugars are great, I'm sleeping
better than in years, my joint aches are gone.

Janice

Not only did Janice drop 11lbs in just five days, but she also got her blood sugar levels in check. This, according to many experts, is impossible on a juice programme due to the apparent high concentration of sugars in the juice. I will cover this later in the book, but not all sugars are equal and *freshly extracted* juice is extremely good at balancing blood sugar, contrary to popular belief. This woman is also sleeping better, her joint aches are gone and she's a happy camper. This has all been achieved, let's not forget, in just five days. We need to understand that these results aren't simply down to the juice, but rather to the unique combination of the absence of *any* rubbish coming into the body while at the same time it's being flooded by nature's finest in liquid form. As I will repeat and repeat throughout this whole book: remove the toxicity and replace the nutrient deficiencies and you give your body a genuine chance to heal.

★　　★　　★

I have tried to lose weight for almost 10 years now. **All I'd read about was low fat, low carb, high protein diet approaches ... that was the supposed magic formula for weight-loss ... never worked for me. I knew the first day in this was going to work. I'm down 10lbs and will stay the course until I lose another 15.** I'm 100 per cent confident it will happen. **I feel great; my skin is better than ever, I sleep so well.**

Margaret

Dropped 10lbs, feeling great, skin better than ever and sleeping well. I would say that one of the most common emails I get is about sleep. We should never underestimate just how much a lack of sleep can affect every aspect of our life and if you do suffer from insomnia, do the programme – it will change your world.

★   ★   ★

Feeling tired is normal, well I thought it was, until I tried the 5lb in 5 days! **When people say they sleep better whilst juicing you just wouldn't believe how fantastic this really is and waking up totally invigorated with the cloud/brain fog totally lifted as if a ray of light was shining on your mind and literally on your head. Amazing. Losing 7lbs was a minor, but lovely, little extra.** Plus I had my [personal best] running a 5k while on juice and significant [personal best] at that. Forgot to mention how great and clean I felt on the inside too!

Andrea

I am hoping this programme will smash many nutritional myths; none more so than the notion that we need crazy amounts of food before and after we exercise. I personally ran the New York and London Marathons on nothing but fresh juice. I also take part in the Great North Run (the largest half marathon in the world) each year and again I run this on juice. The first time I ever did my seven-day juice programme I ran a half marathon on Day 6, in my fastest time ever. On our retreats we do anything from two to five hours' worth of exercise a day, while consuming nothing but fresh juice.

*   *   *

Day 6 of the 5-day plan and I am pretty stunned at the results: **11lbs lost. It's bloomin' amazing. To think I didn't want to juice before because I thought that juice was fattening.** I just needed educating! I am going straight on to do the 5-2-5 plan.

Mimi

I mentioned at the start of this book that the vast majority of people drop far more than the 5lbs in five days advertised, and here is another example of that. For many it would take a couple of months to achieve the same results on a conventional 'calorie-controlled' diet. Not only has this programme effectively turned months into weeks, or into just five days to be accurate, but also it has inspired this lady to want to experience more of the same. I will explain what the 5-2-5 extension plan is all about later (and no, it's not the

5/2 diet!), but what these five days do more than anything else is give you that fire inside again. You will also notice that this woman was under the same misunderstanding which many currently have: that juice is fattening. This is once again based on the misleading information put forward by many dieticians and doctors that 'all sugars are the same and therefore juices will make you fat'. THIS IS SIMPLY NOT TRUE, as this email and thousands like it illustrate.

★   ★   ★

I have lost 5lbs and 2in off my waist and that is with only exercising 5 times. I feel lighter and cleaner on the inside. **Pain from my osteoarthritis and fibromyalgia is nearly gone. Rosacea is cleared, whites of eyes are brighter and a nice natural colour to my lips …
No going back.**

Lynette

Osteoarthritis and fibromyalgia nearly gone and rosacea cleared in just five days. I am not suggesting for one second that this is some kind of miracle cure for all disease, or that if you have these conditions you will get the same results, but this is the type of thing that is happening all over the world as we speak. This 'detox/diet' is not simply about rapid healthy weight loss, but a way to give the body a chance to heal *naturally*.

★   ★   ★

Adult acne now GONE. Happy days! We had to travel to the USA for 5 days a week or so ago and without a juicer and staying at a hotel and hospital (for our son) the food choice was awful ... So the acne started coming back. But since being home almost a week it's gone again. Juicing is the way ...

Denise

I used to be covered in psoriasis; I also had bad eczema and am more than fully aware of what it's like to live with a skin condition. My psoriasis covered my neck and face and it's no picnic living with that, I know. I personally managed to clear my skin by removing all the rubbish in my diet and putting in what nature intended in juice form. My skin took a while to clear as psoriasis is a bugger to shift, but here we have a case where this person's acne went in just five days. I don't wish to give any false hope to those with this condition, but this is pretty incredible and once again shows the healing power of the body once it's given the chance and the right tools to work with.

★   ★   ★

Not only am I down 7.5 pounds but I feel fantastic! My mental clarity and patience has improved so much ... And the BEST part is I quit smoking! I quit cold turkey when I started [juicing] ... and haven't looked back since. I was so preoccupied juicing that I didn't even think about smoking.

Shannon

Another person down over 7lbs in just five days; once again illustrating the 'condense success' nature of this programme. Clearly the biggest side benefit this person had wasn't the weight loss, but the fact they stopped smoking! This isn't the first time I have heard this either; I have had many letters over the years claiming the same. If you do smoke, please don't necessarily expect this to happen to you, but as nicotine only takes three days to leave the body and the actual withdrawal is no more powerful than that of caffeine, why not kick the cigarettes into touch for the next five days and see what happens after that?

★   ★   ★

10.5lbs down ... Yeowwww! To celebrate my clearer skin, better mood and bags of energy I had a banana berry crunch! Yum. Even my hubby and work colleagues noticed a change in me; think the word glow was used!

Caroline

Clearer skin, better mood, glowing inside and out, and down over 10lbs in just five days. Not bad, methinks.

★   ★   ★

Lost 7lbs this week on the 5-day juice programme. In total, 41lbs gone since I started back [9 months ago], just a pound off 3 stone. Dropped 3 dress sizes, skin looks amazing, and it's so great to be a size 12 again ...

Joeli

Later in the book I will strip away all of the usual false arguments against juice diets, one of which is that once you finish the diet you will simply gain all the weight again. Many medical professionals claim it is not a sustainable way to long-term weight loss. This email is just one of thousands I have that says otherwise.

*   *   *

Well I feel like I've accomplished a lot this week: **I lost 11 lbs in 5 days!** A lot of people said I'd didn't have it to lose when I mentioned that I was doing it, but obviously I did! (I am 6ft and reasonably slim). I did the 7 in 7 in January and lost 9lbs, but I exceeded that this week! I teach Pilates over 45 hrs week and have inspired a lot of my clients to try juicing! I love that juicing keeps me focusing on what I put in my body.

Christina

This lady did the 7lbs programme in January and dropped 9lbs in seven days; this time she lost a massive 11lbs in just five days. This is why I developed this programme. By removing one juice a day and adding in my SAB training (coming later) she condensed success and managed better results in fewer days, plus she got his weekend back!

*   *   *

I weighed myself last Tuesday night and was 19st 11lb (277lbs). This morning, 18st 5lbs. **Yep 1st 5lb. (19lbs). WOW. That took me 6 weeks on my last diet!** I cannot believe in 4lbs time I will be the lightest I have been in about 15/16 years.

Greg

This man dropped 19lbs on the seven-day juice programme. I wanted to add his story to this book to illustrate a very important point. Clearly this man didn't lose 19lbs of fat, but he is 19lbs lighter than he was a week ago. All the body is ever looking to do is heal. By removing the junk coming in and replacing it with only the pure 'live' nutrient-filled juice contained within nature's fruits and vegetables, the body can go into healing mode. This man was 277lbs; his body was not designed to be that weight, and was always looking for an opportunity to 'detoxify' itself. This is why in such a short period of time he had such dramatic weight loss. The body was finally given a chance to let go of unwanted crap, and did just that.

The weight loss was clearly not all fat, but it wasn't muscle either; it was the body doing whatever it can to remove the 'danger' to its very survival. When all the junk coming in was removed, the liver, kidneys, lungs and bowel could finally get to work and do what they are always looking to do; remove the rubbish and heal the body. The removal of junk leaves the organs open to do their job and the juices can get on with helping the healing process by providing key nutrients. It also took this man over six weeks to achieve the same level of weight loss last time. As I mentioned at the beginning, I'm all

about 'condensed success' and turning months into weeks –
this is exactly what happened here.

★   ★   ★

My first experience of a juice detox and I am totally
hooked; **I lost ten pounds and feel fantastic, calmer, no
more sugar cravings, am craving healthier foods, slept
better, more energy and can't wait for my next juice ...**
It has transformed my life. Thank you so much.

Rebecca

This email represents thousands of similar ones with the same
message. It is not simply about the initial weight loss (although
10lbs is not to be sneezed at!) but how your cravings change at
the end. '... No more sugar cravings, am craving healthier
foods ...' – isn't that the Holy Grail? Isn't that what we
ultimately want, to change our cravings for junk into actually
wanting healthy food? I get this more than anything else, and
what you think you will be craving at the end of the juice
detox is not what you actually crave. This lady also reported
she felt fantastic, had more energy and was sleeping better.

★   ★   ★

I feel alive! Shadows under my eyes are gone, athletes'
foot clearing up, more energy and a clear head. Just
come back from my first gym session in 6 years. **I've lost
about 7lb and my body fat has gone done to 22 per cent.**

Hannah

This is also extremely common: dark circles or shadows under the eyes disappearing. Dark circles under the eyes can be a sign of tiredness, lack of sleep, fatigue, stress or lack of fresh air. On the other hand, it can also indicate a more serious illness, and is connected with heart, kidneys, thyroid gland or metabolic illnesses. But for this juicer, the shadows under her eyes are completely gone – how come? Because, as I will constantly repeat, the body just wants to heal! Please also notice that her athletes' foot is also clearing up. The reason I wanted to point this out is because many people think juice feeds yeast and therefore should be avoided by anyone with Candida or conditions like athletes' foot. This is not the case with the *freshly extracted* fruit and vegetable juices in this programme.

★   ★   ★

Day 8 and I am so chuffed as have lost 11lbs and 2in from my waist and hips! The weight loss is great but I am so, so very pleased that my health has improved. Not so much chest pain because of the angina, my BP is normal and stable, my GFR count is rising, I am breathing better and easier, my joints are not so swollen, and I am not suffering as much with the fibromyalgia ...

Lynne

Where do we start? Tremendous weight loss, improved angina, blood pressure normal, GFR rate up (that's Glomerular filtration rate, which is the best estimate of kidney function), she's breathing better (the freshly extracted apple juice is wonderful for that), joints not as swollen and not suffering as much with her fibromyalgia. Once again so many apparent 'different' ailments improving all at the same time, One disease – one solution!

★　　　★　　　★

I didn't do this for weight loss as was only 8st 4lb. Although I have lost 3lb the most important thing is that before doing this I hadn't been able to kneel down for over a year as my knees were swollen with arthritis! **Seven days on nutrient-filled juice and the swelling has gone and I can now kneel down.** Woo hoo, over a year of pain and swelling GONE!

Emma

This woman wasn't able to kneel down for over a year as her knees were swollen with arthritis and in one week on the juice the swelling has gone and she can kneel. Remove the rubbish, replace the nutrients and you change the internal environment so the body can heal ... naturally.

★　　　★　　　★

I've cleared up my eczema on my hands to the point where I no longer feel the need to have long sleeves. We both have more energy, life seems clearer, I'm calmer, sleep better, happier, more confident, the list goes on ... in terms of weight loss ... I lost 9 pound and hubby lost 10 pound.

Donna

I am more than aware of what it feels like not to wear short sleeves and always having to cover up due to a skin problem. To clear it to the point where this lady feels she can now be free to wear what she wants in just one week is truly spectacular. I am not suggesting this would happen to everyone with eczema, but it did for her. Not only did her skin improve, both her and her husband reported having more energy and feeling that life seems clearer; they're calmer, sleep better and feel more confident. This is all within a week!

★   ★   ★

9lbs lost, 6 inches down, and **body fat lowered by 3 per cent** on day 8! Sleeping great, skin feels better ... I couldn't achieve this in a year, so to do it in a week is amazing!

Melissa

That's 3 per cent reduction in body fat, which is quite remarkable in a week, and flies in the face of what many believe is possible. Over the years I have received hundreds of emails reporting similar or better fat percentage reductions; one person even said they had stripped their body fat by 5 per cent ... in a week.

★   ★   ★

Well 9.9lbs for me and 8.8lbs for Marc! Woweeeee. What's more, **my depression has lifted**! I have been depressed for nearly four years, but it has left the building! I'm sleeping better, my hubby doesn't snore anymore! We are converted! I've got my life back.

Siobhan

You cannot heal selectively, which is why everything seems to get better on both a physical and mental level. I think the nutrients found in good quality fruits and vegetables are the key to giving the brain, as well as the body, what it ultimately needs for optimum health.

★　　★　　★

Wow, the end of an incredible week. Can't wait for my juice tomorrow morning :-) **Skin feels great, lost inches all over, hair soft, asthma better, IBS gone!**

Clare

Skin great, lost inches, hair soft, asthma better and IBS gone; 'one disease – one solution' in action once again.

★　　★　　★

Are you starting to notice a pattern here? Are you starting to see that the health possibilities go way beyond dropping a few pounds? I wish to make this clear to those sceptics (as there are many out there) – I haven't received a dozen or two of these testimonials. I've received tens of thousands of them, all reporting incredible positive health changes in exceptionally short periods of time. There are simply too many to be dismissed as just anecdotal evidence.

A PILL FOR EVERY ILL AND AN ILL FOR EVERY PILL

What became very clear to me early on when the letters and emails started flooding in was just how many apparent 'different' ailments and diseases improved at the same time. The medical profession's focus tends to be on 'a pill for every ill' philosophy and they try to treat each ailment or disease separately with different pills. What appears to be obvious to me now, is that when you remove *all* of the rubbish coming in and flood the body with the right nutrients to address any vitamin, mineral or other nutrient deficiencies, *everything* has a chance to heal. I didn't take a specific juice to treat my asthma, eczema, hay fever, psoriasis or obesity; I simply removed all of the rubbish coming in and flooded my body with the finest nutrients in the most bio-available form – fresh juice.

I also wish to point out at this stage that I am all for intelligent, and often much needed, short-term, and at rare times, long-term medical intervention. I also don't believe that every single disease will be cured or made better by a fresh juice. However, the vast majority of common *lifestyle* diseases, the ones we are popping pills like they are going out of fashion for, do indeed get better when you treat with fresh natural juices.

This 'one disease – one solution' hypothesis is not simply based on my own experience. It is based on the tens of thousands of testimonials I've had over the years and from what I have personally seen at my retreats for years. I am convinced that if you remove *all* the rubbish coming into the body and address all of the nutritional deficiencies, the vast majority of lifestyle diseases will either improve dramatically or go away completely. This is an intelligent hunch based on 15 years' worth of research.

I put this 'hunch' to the test in my *Super Juice Me!* documentary: a group of people with over 22 apparent diseases living on nothing but juice for 28 days. Trust me, it makes interesting viewing – and the results will blow your mind! I am hoping in time it will start to affect the way the medical profession approach healing and disease.

I think this is still a long way off, unfortunately. But, the more people start shouting from the rooftops about how great they feel after getting rid of all the rubbish going into their body, while flooding their system with the finest plant nutrients through fresh juice, the more they will have to sit up and take notice.

Luckily, it is not lost on all in the medical profession and things are starting to change. More and more are understanding that nature's finest nutrient-packed liquid fuel contains something often way beyond any human or scientific understanding. More and more people in the medical profession are no longer relying on the 'evidence' produced by the pharmaceutical reps, who bombard them with the latest drug that can cure obesity as well as just about every common ailment. They are using common sense and starting to believe in the power of plant-based foods and the body's ability to naturally heal itself. I am not anti-doctor; a doctor has even written the foreword for this book, but I am anti *certain* doctors and *certain* dieticians who, despite what thousands are reporting, still close their minds to any plant-based 'food as medicine' approach to healing. The good news is though, it's not all doctors and the message is slowly filtering through:

Hi Jason,

I'm a GP, for my sins, and have been following your programmes for the last 2 months, prompted by a serious illness in January that left me unable to eat anything except juices and smoothies. I've lost over 2 stone (28lbs) in that time and am now telling patients about it. It's working for me whereas in the past other diets (rather than changes in lifestyle, as this is) have not ... I think this is something that is realistic and that people can do. I've never eaten as much fruit and veg in my life, and am enjoying it and also am full on it. My type 1 diabetes control is improving ...

On a professional note, people far prefer to take a tablet (which is easy) than do something hard like totally change their lifestyle. I will continue to advocate you to patients and colleagues – I know I'm only one GP amongst thousands but every little helps I guess.

Kate

And yes, every little does help, as people tend to listen to what a doctor has to say on the subject of nutrition. You may feel that's an intelligent thing to do, but it's worth knowing that the average doctor in the UK spends just three to six *hours* of their six *years* of training studying nutrition. No, I am not kidding.

The good news is you don't need to spend years studying the fundamentals of nutrition in order to know what to do to have a slim, trim, energy-driven, ailment-free body. I have been studying health and nutrition for over 15 years and I have realized one thing more than any other: the more I study the less I know. What I mean is, we have so overcomplicated the issue of health and disease we have missed the simplicity of it. We have missed just how stupidly straightforward the answer to health can be. Do you remember when you were a kid and fell and cut your knee, what was the advice? 'Leave it alone and it will heal itself.' And that is all we need to do – give the body the right environment to be in a position to heal itself.

Part 1

THE TRUTH ABOUT JUICING

GOOD THINGS COME TO THOSE WHO WAIT

By now you should be itching to get started – PLEASE DON'T! There are a few things that need addressing first to make sure you are fully armed for anything that comes your way. The last thing you want to do is buy a load of fruit and veg to find it making its own way out of the fridge later in the week! You don't want to start something and then fail and you are far less likely to fail if you are equipped with the right mental tools before you start.

To be honest, it seems insane that I even need to cover the following points, but after doing this for years, I know that unless I do people who don't know any better will try and scare you off doing the programme. What you will hear (and you may even be asking these questions to yourself as you read this book) are things like, 'What about all the sugar in the juices?', 'Where will you get your fibre?', 'Where will you get your protein?', 'Won't you just gain the weight back again?', and so on.

All of these questions will be covered in this part of the book, but as I write this very sentence, as if by fate, I have just seen a famous UK TV doctor talking about my juice diets! (Yes, how weird!)He was banging on with the usual rhetoric, such as 'it's unhealthy', 'it can be dangerous' and so on (which is all nonsense and which I will cover soon), but he also once again made a bold statement that I cannot ignore and one which I have heard many people in the medical profession level at me before …

Detox
IS A
MYTH

3

The TV doc's exact words were:

> Complete myth, there is no such thing as detox; it's
> absolute rubbish. You have three perfectly good organs,
> your liver and two kidneys, which do all the detoxing
> you need ...

Technically, our TV doc has a point – the body does indeed detoxify itself with the help of its perfectly good organs designed to do precisely that. I am also fully aware that fresh juice doesn't detox the body *per se*; only the body, essentially, detoxs the body. However, there are two fundamental points our TV doc, and many others, are missing when it comes to the word 'detox'.

Firstly, just because the body wants and is designed to do certain things naturally, it doesn't mean it's always in the position to do so. Take breathing for example; the body naturally wants to breathe; its very survival depends on it. However, if someone were to put their hands around your neck and start to lightly squeeze, or if you were caught up in a house fire, the body would have much greater difficulty doing what it naturally, and desperately, wants to do. Equally, if a person constantly puts more toxicity (refined sugars, fats, salts, alcohol, nicotine, etc.) into the body than it can detoxify (or eliminate if you will) efficiently, then it will struggle doing what it naturally was designed, and is desperate, to do.

If, as the TV doc suggests:

'... you have three perfectly good organs, your liver and two kidneys, which do all the detoxing you need ...'

then, by that rationale, there is no need to stop smoking, curb heavy drinking, or cut down on junk food for that matter, as the body will do *all* the detoxing for you.

It is more than clear that our detoxifying organs cannot always cope with the amount of toxicity coming in and they are not capable of doing *all* the detoxifying for us if overburdened. If they did, then no matter what we put in we would all be slim and healthy for life, and people like my beautiful mother wouldn't have passed away so prematurely from stage 4 lung cancer due to the toxic nature of tobacco; her lungs would have simply detoxed it out. The more rubbish you pile into your body in the absence of *live* high-water content nutrient-rich foods and drinks, the more the organs have difficulty coping. Stop putting in the rubbish and, then yes, the body will indeed detoxify itself. So I agree that the body is essentially the only thing which technically detoxifies the body. I also agree that juicing *per se* does not detoxify the body. However, by eliminating all the toxic rubbish from one's diet and supplying the system with freshly extracted juices, the body will then be free to do what it naturally wants and needs to do every minute of every day – detoxify!

WHAT'S IN A WORD?

Secondly, the vast majority of people will be doing this five-day juice-only detox to lose weight and kick-start a healthy lifestyle. They don't think the juices will act in place of their perfectly good detoxing organs such as the liver and kidneys and nor do they think that is what the word means. And this is perhaps the biggest point to be made here. The *vast* majority of people use and understand the word 'detox' to mean

The Elimination of Certain Foods and Drinks for a Set Period of Time.

They understand it to be a set period of time where they abstain from things such as caffeine, refined sugars, refined fats, alcohol and so on. Who honestly ever really thinks that 'juice detox' means anything other than that? Well, apart from some doctors and scientists of course, but here in 'normal world' the meaning on the ground has changed and they need to catch up.

This book is entitled *5-Day Juice Challenge: The Juice Detox Diet*, not because of my lack of understanding of how the body actually works, but rather because 99.99 per cent of people who pick it up know exactly what that means. They won't think juices detoxify the body, but rather that they will have a period of time without certain foods and drinks while drinking nothing but juice.

The meaning of some words change over time anyway, and sometimes if used enough in a certain way, end up meaning the complete opposite of what the actual definition is. Take the word 'bad', for example. I grew up in a place called Peckham in southeast London where if you said a certain piece of music or a film or even an item of clothing was 'bad'; it actually meant it was 'good'. It is now widely understood that if someone refers to certain things as 'bad' they actually mean 'good'. Clearly it's not the actual meaning of bad in the dictionary, but it has changed and that's just how it is. If something is really good some people now refer to it as 'sick', but anybody using this term doesn't actually believe for a millisecond that an item of clothing can projectile vomit! So if you get anyone saying: 'Detox is a myth', please tell them to stop being so flipping pedantic, as they are more than fully aware of what you and I mean by the word.

Having said that, I have just looked up the Oxford English Dictionary's definition of 'detox' and it appears it is indeed what we all believe it to be rather than what the TV doc suggests.

detox informal noun, Pronunciation: [mass noun].
a process or period of time in which one abstains from or rids the body of toxic or unhealthy substances.

This is exactly what this programme is: a period of time, five days to be exact, where 'one abstains from or rids the body of toxic or unhealthy substances'. Where's the confusion? And moreover what is the problem with calling it a 'detox' when that is exactly what it is? If 'Detox is a myth', as the TV doc stated on national television, then perhaps it should be removed from the Oxford English Dictionary?

Once you've addressed the fact that 'detox diet' is indeed a perfectly reasonable phrase for this five-day programme, you'll have another couple of big guns to contend with from the juice sceptics out there. Please also remember you are not simply dealing with genuine sceptics either, but also with friends and family members who may not overly want you get slim and healthy while they aren't doing so! That sounds terrible, but it's the way of the world. After all, if your next-door neighbour renovates their house and makes it look amazing, in order to make your house look good you have a couple of choices. You can either make an effort to renovate your house too, or you can blow their house up! Many people who feel they cannot make a change in this area for whatever reason will, consciously or sub-consciously, do anything to prevent you from 'doing your house up', so to speak. This is why they will often attack what you are doing; it's simply in order to prevent you from doing it so your house stays in the same condition as theirs. If you make your house look amazing it only brings attention to how bad theirs is.

Fear, of course, is the most common approach used by both genuine juice sceptics, and the many friends who don't want your house to improve. This is why many say, 'it's dangerous' and why you will hear the following arguments. I am adding these to the book for one reason alone, to arm you with the right information so you are not scared away from doing this programme.

How anyone can think that drinking freshly extracted vegetable and fruit juice for just five days is in any way, shape or form harmful is one of life's great mysteries. However, somehow they can be convincing and many people don't try this on for size because they listen to the nonsense without questioning it. You can live on water for five days and all would be OK, so the fears are completely unfounded, but let's debunk them anyway before we start. I have heard the first one for over 15 years, and it's one of the first things people argue when talking about juice detox diets.

What About ALL THE SUGAR?

4

The Sugar in an Apple Is
Not the Same
As the Sugar in a Doughnut!

And the sugar in fizzy drinks is not the same as the sugar in a *freshly extracted* apple juice! You may feel this doesn't need covering. You may feel that it's obvious that the white refined *nutrient-stripped sugar* found in a doughnut and a fizzy drink is clearly not the same as the unrefined vitamin, mineral and *soluble fibre-rich* 'sugar' found in an apple and the fresh juice extracted from it. But ever since the late Dr Robert Atkins' famous 'don't eat carbs whatever you do or you'll explode' diet (I believe this is better known as a high-protein diet) and all the subsequent copies of pretty much *exactly* the same theme since then, such as the Dukan diet, it appears our rational thinking has taken a holiday. My mother always taught me, 'the problem with common sense is that it isn't that common', and I fear where the subject of sugar is concerned, for many, it's disappeared completely.

Most people are so over-read in the area of diet and nutrition that often they don't stop to use their common sense; they simply believe what they read and preach it as gospel. This is why I don't want you to simply buy what I am saying either; always have an open mind and if something makes rational sense to you, then apply it; if not – don't. But don't simply go along with a school of thought simply because it was written or told to you by a doctor or dietician, or because it's been 'scientifically proven'. Often we don't need science, but our own intuition and common sense.

WHERE'S THE WATER?

Somehow, Atkins and co managed to convince millions of people that bacon and eggs in a frying pan are better for us than an apple – a legacy that still remains to this day. But what does your genuine intuition tell you? Over 92 per cent of the planet is made of water (72 per cent of its surface), over 70 per cent of our bodies are made of it and without it no life on earth would exist. Its importance, I feel, is undisputed. Every single fruit and vegetable designed for human consumption is made up of over 80 per cent pure organic rich water; many fruits and vegetables contain over 90 per cent. This water is designed to transport the essential nutrients within plant food to every cell in the body, while at the same time this essential water helps to flush out any rubbish. We have over 30 feet worth of intestinal tract, designed specifically for high-water-content foods. This water is not only essential for transporting key nutrients and helping to flush the body of toxicity, it also enriches the skin. In my opinion, there are many down sides on the health front to things like the Atkins Diet, but none more so than that gaunt look. You know, that look of total dehydration, like a withered plant that you just want to water.

We're not meant to be stick thin, we're not meant to avoid water-rich foods and we are most certainly not meant to avoid the sugar found in nature's finest life-giving fruits and vegetables! How we have reached the stage where people honestly believe an apple is worse for their health than fried bacon is beyond me, but we have and that is why I'm having to write this chapter. The belief that the sugars in fruit and vegetable juices are the same as those in a can of fizzy drink are so strong now that I feel I really must put this to bed. I will do this not through 'science' but with an often-unused foolproof method – intuition and common sense.

TAKE THE FRIDGE TEST

With this in mind let me ask you a question. If you were a genuine sugar addict and you had a mother of a sugar craving, would an organic apple cut it for you? Would an apple hit those sugar craving buttons for you? Would you leave the house to go hunting for your apple fix? NO! Why? Because:

The Sugar in an Apple Is Not the Same As the Sugar in a Doughnut!

If it were, we would have Easter eggs made of fruit and children and adults would be just as happy, but they wouldn't be, because in the same way an apple wouldn't satisfy a smoker's need for nicotine, an apple wouldn't satisfy a sugar addict's desire for *refined* sugars! It's *refined* sugars and *refined* fats that are the biggest cause of preventable lifestyle diseases in the western world and without question they are the biggest cause of the seemingly unstoppable obesity epidemic. It is *not* the unrefined vitamin, mineral and soluble fibre-rich juice found at the heart of all nature's finest foods.

This is why you could have a fridge entirely full of fruit and vegetables and the average sugar addict would still say, 'where's the food?' Unless there is *refined* sugar or *refined* fat in the mix, they feel as though what's in the fridge just won't cut it. Their eyes will scan everywhere for bread, chips, crisps, chocolate, fizzy drinks, muffins, waffles, biscuits, etc. In other words, *anything* containing the types of sugars and fats that will curb their cravings. Broccoli, kale, carrots, apples, spinach, celery, avocados, cucumber will not excite them as their types of sugars and fats are not the same and will not curb their cravings!

It's also why although there's an NA (Narcotics Anonymous), an AA (Alcoholics Anonymous), and even an SA (Sugar Anonymous), you will never see an FA (Fruit Anonymous), or a VA (Vegetable Anonymous). People just aren't hooked on cucumber, avocado or apples despite their apparent high sugar content. You will not find a FEJA (Freshly Extracted Juice Anonymous) either. Why? Because, and I am fully aware of how annoying repetition can be, so for the final time: **the sugar in fruit is not the same as the sugar in a doughnut.**

It's also why if someone were to eat apples all their lives and suddenly went on a 'no apple diet' they wouldn't get headaches, anxiety, the shakes or any of the other withdrawal symptoms people experience when trying to break a *refined* sugar addiction. One sugar is pure and comes attached with a multitude of other micronutrients and soluble fibre, and the other is stripped of its goodness and has effectively been transformed into a drug-like substance. Plastic and petrol are both by-products of crude oil, but nobody in their right mind would suggest you could run your car by putting cut-up plastic in your tank! However, the 'all sugars are the same' brigade often miss this fundamental point. They miss that a food like broccoli is much, much more than the carbohydrate 'sugar' contained within.

They also miss the fact that it's possible that humans don't fully understand the huge complexities of nutrition that are contained within the natural foods nature provides. After all, nature simply intended to give us the means to grow them and eat them; I doubt if she ever knew the degree to which every element would be studied in the future. Wild animals never study their food; they just eat it and go. And I guess that is the biggest problem; humans think they know everything about everything and believe they have discovered every element worth knowing about in nature's foods. Some of the top scientists continue to believe this despite the fact that new photochemicals are being found all the time in fruits and vegetables. I read recently that scientists are confident they know about 60–70 per cent of what's in an apple. They admit they don't know all of what's in it, as there are thousands of phytonutrients that haven't been named or even found yet, but they are confident they know about 60–70 per cent. But how on earth can you possibly think you know you have found any percentage if you don't know what the 100 per cent looks like? I cannot tell you I know what 60 per cent of the nutrition in an apple is if I don't know what 100 per cent is, can I?!

If all sugars are equal and 'juice diets are full of sugar', which we hear all the time, then why do some people still have sugar cravings during the first few days of a fresh juice diet? Why do they still experience sugar withdrawal despite the level of juices going into the body?

Many scientists, doctors and dieticians continue to believe that all sugars are the same, despite knowing that every single nutrient reacts differently in the body depending what it is combined with. Isn't it possible, and again I'm just throwing it out there, that we don't know everything about the tens of thousands of different and unique nutrients found in the liquid of all fruits and vegetables, and that just because the 'science' of today says something is so, it doesn't necessarily make it so?

Venice A. Fulton, author of *Six Weeks to OMG: Get Skinnier Than All of Your Friends*, another 'new' high protein diet, claims that the carbohydrates in broccoli can be as bad for slimmers as Coca-Cola. Nope, I am not kidding. All fruits and vegetables are at least 85 per cent nutrient rich in water and it's this juice and this juice alone that feeds every cell in the body. It is this water which contains not only the sugars, or natural carbohydrates as I prefer to call them, but also the potassium, magnesium, calcium, zinc, phosphorus, iron, sodium, vitamins A, B, C, E, K and the tens of thousands of other nutrients and co-factors which all go to make up this remarkable liquid fuel. To suggest drinking a juice is the same as drinking a fizzy drink, which has an average of eight teaspoons of white refined sugar in just one can, along with a whole host of other chemicals, is about as far removed from common sense as you can get.

YES, BUT ISN'T JUICE HIGH G.I. (GLYCEMIC INDEX)?

Once we get passed the 'all sugars are the same' debate we hit the G.I. argument. So while I am here, let's put this to bed too. Yes, 'cooked' juice, or *pasteurized* as it is more commonly known, is indeed high G.I. However, what many don't realize is that although pasteurized apple juice (which is every juice you buy in a carton or bottle) has a high G.I., *freshly extracted apple juice* made at home has a low G.I. Not that G.I. is any real indicator of how good or bad a food or drink is anyway. Like many fads, the whole Glycemic Index trend, and subsequent G.L. (Glycemic Load) diets, have more holes than your average colander. For example, no two people will react in exactly the same way to a particular carbohydrate, so you would have to test each person separately to see if *that* particular food or drink had an adverse sugar spike reaction on *that* particular individual. The reaction will also be different depending on what that particular food or drink has been consumed with. Like most scientific scales of this nature, it tends to have not been terribly well thought through and yet it gets treated as gospel. Everyone then starts looking at foods and drinks to see where they are on the G.I. scale when it's about as effective as a cat flap in a hippo house. It's like the BMI scale (Body Mass Index), another 'scientific scale' which claims to determine if someone is overweight, obese or morbidly obese. Many athletes are obese according to this scale, because BMI doesn't take into account muscle.

WHAT'S UP WITH A LITTLE 'LIGHT' PASTURIZATION?

If I were to take your head and stick it in an oven and 'lightly pasteurize' it at 100°C for one minute, your head would no longer be the same. Yes, you'd still have your ears, nose, mouth and eyes, but they wouldn't be able to function in the same way! Likewise, when you take an apple and apply that kind of heat you change its molecular structure and it no longer functions in the same way. The tens of thousands of delicate phytonutrients and enzymes are changed … forever. It is no longer what nature had in mind for you and your trillions of cells. This is also why the slower the juicer, in terms of extracting your juice from fruits and vegetables, the better; slower juicers create less heat friction. However, even if you have a high-speed juicer it will not turn freshly extracted juice into cooked juice as pasteurization does.

BUT WHAT ABOUT ALL THE FRUCTOSE?

Many who raise the sugar argument also talk about the high concentration of the new sugar evil on the block: fructose. When I was growing up I was under the impression that fructose was the sugar found *only* in fruits and vegetables and glucose was the sugar you add to your coffee and cereal. You will of course find fructose, sucrose and glucose to varying degrees in just about anything containing sugar, including fruit and vegetables. This isn't something we need to get bogged down with, although many people do, but it's worth pointing out that white refined table sugar, the sugar the vast majority of people consume, is loaded with fructose. Unfortunately, this doesn't get shouted from the rooftops when people get all anti-fructose. For some reason, this white, refined, nutrition-free, fibre-free, table sugar never appears to get the hammering for the overconsumption of fructose in today's world. Neither does High Fructose Corn Syrup (HFCS). Instead, once again fruit and vegetable juices take the rap!

HFCS is now the sugar of choice for a great deal of BIG FOOD and BIG DRINK companies when sweetening their wares, especially in the good ole US of A, as it's very, very cheap to produce. It is also very high in fructose, as the name suggests. Fructose, like all sugars, when everything else around it has been stripped away, can indeed be extremely harmful.

This is why people are now freaking out about juices. However, unlike table sugar and HFCS, freshly extracted fruit and vegetable juices are a great deal more than just the fructose they contain. They contain plenty of rich soluble fibre and a very high concentration of phytonutrients, as well as enzymes, and numerous other co-factors which haven't been identified yet. This all means that the sugars in juices are metabolized differently from the completely empty white refined sugar, HFCS and others of the same ilk.

I wholeheartedly agree that drinking shedloads of *pasteurized* orange juice can potentially have a negative effect, and cause many of the issues people who shout 'watch out for the sugar in juices' say they do. I also agree that *very high concentrations* of fructose in table sugar and HFCS are, in many people's opinion, including my own, responsible for the vast majority of lifestyle diseases humans suffer from today. There is also no question that HFCS, white refined table sugar and even pasteurized juices are all potential precursors to type 2 diabetes and obesity. If I were advising anyone with type 2 diabetes on what to eat and drink I would immediately take table sugar, HFCS and *cooked* juices off the table, but (and it's a big but), I would 100 per cent leave in freshly extracted vegetable juices, what I call green blends (fruit and vegetable juices blended with avocado) and, to a smaller extent, fruit juices.

Why? Because they are simply not the same as the heat-blasted versions. I know science will argue otherwise, and I know there will be many doctors, dieticians and scientists jumping up and down and screaming at this page, but I can guarantee that the science on this will change, as it did with the science about fat being the root of all obesity and diabetes evil. If you wrote anything in favour of fat and suggested that it was sugar that was the problem back in the 1970s and

1980s, 'science' would have been against you. I don't have the science to back me up yet on this one, but I have 15 years' experience in using freshly extracted juice and green blends to help people with obesity, diabetes and conditions like thrush, in which sugar is known to be one of the biggest causes and aggravators. If all sugars were indeed the same, and cooked juices and live juices were the same, and fructose were the apparent cause of these problems, then why do these conditions improve so much on my programmes? I have received thousands of genuine heartfelt messages from people all over the world whose results fly in the face of the 'all sugars are the same' argument; many saying how their diabetes improved, which shouldn't happen if the fructose in fruit and vegetable juices is the bad boy as claimed.

Here's just one example. This is a guy who came on my retreat with diabetes and reduced his insulin by 75 per cent in just one week, something which wouldn't happen with a week on fizzy drinks, crisps and muffins!

John's insulin was reduced by two thirds having spent just 1 week with you at Juicy Oasis and we have just received his annual checkup results:
Reduction of insulin maintained, cholesterol back to normal after 7 years (unbelievable), continued weight loss, blood sugar levels perfect! Thanks for showing us the way.

Jackie and John

If you have diabetes, type 1 especially, always check with your GP before embarking on any programme of this nature as everyone reacts differently, and I am not suggesting for a second that this is a cure for diabetes. But experiences like this once again illustrate the fact that raw 'live' juices, especially when veggie-based and blended with avocado, can not only *not* affect these conditions adversely, but can potentially improve them.

If you do get hammered about the 'all the sugar' you will be consuming, please just pass them the book and, in particular, this chapter. That one email should at least help them to start to think differently. Even if you do manage to convince people that the sugar in an apple is indeed not the same as the sugar in a doughnut, the questions and doubts about what you are doing won't stop there. People will fire them at you at such a rate of knots it's almost hard to keep up! So let's strip the rest of the arguments away, starting with perhaps the next big gun in their disapproving chamber ...

What About *THE* FIBRE?

5

When you eat a carrot all that happens is the body does whatever it can to extract the juice contained within the fibres and then it disposes of the waste (the fibre).

Fibre Cannot Penetrate Through the Intestinal Wall, Meaning It Does Not Feed the Body

Yes, we need fibre, and after the initial five days I am not advocating anyone becoming a 'juicearian', so you will easily be getting enough fibre in the regular good food you will be eating after you finish this programme. However, what many do not understand is that you will also be getting plenty of fibre *during* the programme too. Not only does *every* freshly extracted juice in this plan contain 'soluble' fibre, many of the juices also have blended avocado or banana – two of the richest fibre foods on earth. Soluble fibre, which you will be getting mainly through the freshly extracted apple juice (this is why I use it as a base in a great deal of the juices), absorbs water and binds with the digested material in your stomach to create a viscous gel. This helps to 'lift' rubbish from the colon and aids in slowing down the digestive process, which is beneficial because your body has more time to absorb nutrients in your stomach. The regular consumption of soluble fibre food sources also means you may be able to achieve better blood sugar control, which is also why this programme is also OK for the vast majority of type 2 diabetics (always check with your GP, clearly). This is because the gel slows down the rate at which sugar enters the bloodstream, which can help keep energy levels steady.

This comes as a shock to many because many people believe juice is juice and don't understand the incredible differences between 'cooked' juice and freshly extracted juice. Soluble fibre not only helps food move along the gut, but it also lowers cholesterol by binding to it in the gut. This could explain why the cholesterol lowering results from this programme are also off the chart. I have seen people drop 3 points off their cholesterol within just a week. I am hoping one day the medical profession will see there is a very safe, side-effect free, alternative to statins (cholesterol-lowering drugs). Statins are becoming BIG PHARMA'S best friend as they have very quickly become a multi-billion pound industry and the financial generating new kid on the block. Believe it or not, and I wish I was making this up, it has even been suggested that large fast food chains should give out statins when serving burgers; this idea was labelled 'McStatin'. Welcome to twenty-first-century medicine! It was even suggested that statins should be added to our drinking water (by a top professor no less). Luckily there are a handful of freedom-of-choice laws left in Britain so it's not possible to mass medicate without our permission (although that didn't stop Fluoride being added to our drinking water, so statins may indeed be finding their way out of your tap). What is happening though, is that liver-toxic statins are being given to hundreds of thousands of people who don't even have cholesterol issues in a bid to prevent heart disease. This, despite the fact that even according to the pharmaceutical companies' own research (which is often skewed to make the drug look the very best it can be) statins will only extend your life by a *maximum* of 14 days. This of course is all for another time, but I wanted to touch on it here as it illustrates a little of what's happening out there. Right, back to fibre!

It's the Juice Contained Within the Fibres That Feed the Body

This juice programme has been carefully designed so that your morning and evening juices are blended with either avocado or banana, both of which are extremely good sources of insoluble and soluble fibre. I have also added in a 'HUNGER SOS' to the programme, where you are free to eat an apple, avocado, or *very* healthy energy bar a day (details later). This once again adds more than enough fibre to your diet. Having said that, even if none of the freshly extracted juices in this programme contained avocado or banana and you skipped your HUNGER SOS, you would *still* have plenty of soluble fibre. And of course we need to remember it's only for five days! I will put your mind at rest now: you will not have a 'fibre deficiency' and your health will not be negatively affected in just five days on this programme. Anyone who says it will is either simply scaremongering or needs a lesson in nutrition.

These won't be the only arguments you'll hear, trust me. Get prepared for 'Where are you going to get your protein?' Even though

A you won't get a protein deficiency in five days, and

B the juices and green blend smoothies contain amino acids, the very building blocks for protein.

That's before we get onto the fact the largest land animals on earth such as, elephants, bullocks, rhinos, giraffes, etc., are all vegans. These heavily-muscled mammals gain all of their protein requirements from plant-based amino acid-rich foods. Yet, despite this fact, get ready for the fear-based question about protein. And, if I haven't mentioned this enough – IT'S ONLY FOR FIVE DAYS!

Then you'll have 'Where will you get your calcium?' Even though once again:

A you won't get a calcium deficiency in just five days, even if you consume nothing but water!

B all of the juices and smoothies contain certain amounts of this mineral;

C the biggest teeth of any land mammal are those of the bull elephant, which gets all its calcium from plant-based foods; and finally

D it's not just where you are getting your calcium but what's robbing you of it. For five days at least you won't be having refined sugars, caffeine, alcohol or any other highly acidic food or drink, which all rob the body of its calcium stores.

You'll also, as mentioned at the start of this book, get people saying, 'but it's not healthy to lose weight so quickly', and no matter what weight-loss success you have initially it's all pointless because once you start to eat normally …

You'll Only GAIN IT ALL BACK AGAIN

6

The TV doc's actual words were:

> ... going on these crazy juice diets just makes you very, very hungry, usually quite grumpy and miserable, and usually ends up with you putting on more weight when you start to eat normally at the end of it.

It's hard to know where to start here, as nothing could be further than the truth of just about everything he said. The vast majority of people in the UK are now classed as either overweight or obese, suggesting they aren't exactly focused on their daily nutritional needs when they eat 'normally' anyway. It always makes me laugh when I see someone who is the size of the Napa valley asking, 'But where will I get my protein and calcium if I start juicing?' as if this was usually a major concern of theirs! On that note, I see people who usually eat nothing but refined fat, salt and sugar being concerned about the possible pesticides. The few pesticides that may be in the non-organic fruit and veg they buy will seem like a breath of fresh air compared to what they usually shove in!

Please don't lose sleep if you hear any comment from a TV doc, normal doc or random person who says you will have nutritional deficiencies if you do this programme for just five days because it's utter, utter, utter rubbish. The vast majority of people jumping on juice detoxes of this nature are the ones who are already suffering nutritional deficiencies. It's the lack of genuine nutrition which cause the overweight or obese person to constantly feel hungry and overeat. This brings me onto the second part of what he said,

> ... going on these crazy juice diets just makes you very, very hungry, usually quite grumpy and miserable.

I assumed he had interviewed thousands of people who have done my apparent 'crazy juice diets' and come to that conclusion, but alas no. It was simply a statement. The thousands of emails I have received over the years tell a very different story; many mention how surprised they were because they weren't hungry. Most people are overfed and undernourished, which is why they constantly try to fill the void with more of the same empty food that is ironically causing the very problem they are trying to solve. When you juice you supply your body with the finest plant-based nutrients in the best bio-available form, and because the nutrients are in liquid form they are easier for the body to utilize. This means that your cells are indeed being fed, which is why many people are surprised at how easy it can be. The chances of the average person in the UK getting fewer of the nutrients they need by doing this five-day programme are zero!

There are of course some people who do feel hungry, grumpy and miserable, but these don't make up the vast majority and usually it's the people who skipped reading the book and didn't know how to deal with the mental *false hungers* created by the withdrawal from refined sugars and caffeine who suffer. When you drink the juices in this programme you are getting all the nutrients you need and you are being fed. If you feel hungry it's down to *empty withdrawal* from junk foods and drinks, not because you aren't actually feeding yourself! When people come off cigarettes they can also feel miserable and grumpy but this isn't because cigarettes provide something the body genuinely needs for its survival, but rather because they are experiencing *physical* withdrawal from nicotine and feel *mentally* deprived because they cannot smoke anymore. I will cover this in more depth in a later chapter, which will explain exactly how to recognize any false physical hungers so you can, like the vast majority of people, find the five days easy.

The TV doc then finishes with a claim made by many in the 'uninformed about juicing' camp:

> [the juice diet] usually ends up with you putting on more weight when you start to eat normally at the end of it.

Firstly he, like many doctors and dieticians who come out with this point, seems to have done done no research into my book at all, or got in touch with any of the tens of thousands of people who have done the programme. If he had he would have seen all the people who did the programme and went on to reach their ideal weight, and those that went on to change their lifestyle beyond. I think the best way to illustrate this is to share a few more of the tens of thousands of messages I've received; messages that show that, for many people, juicing has become a daily part of their life and that the detox was the springboard to a healthier lifestyle.

> Thank you Jason ... I did the 7-day detox a year ago, as well as this week ... after the first 7 days I lost 10 pounds. By using your common sense approach **I lost the rest of the 55 pounds** and have **kept it off for a year now.** I am 61 years old and only wish that I had become a juicer early in life.
>
> *Leonora*

> Wow ... **Lost so far nearly 2 stone (28lbs) but more importantly my health and energy has gone through the roof ...** I continue to juice everyday Monday to Friday and eat low-cal fresh healthy meals at weekends ... Everyone I see says I look great and I feel amazing and all thanks to Jason Vale Juice Master. You're inspirational and life changing. Thank you!
>
> *Paula*

I have thousands of similar emails from people who went onto to lose a tremendous amount of weight after the 'springboard' juice detox and have kept it off too. I have even seen someone go on to drop over 200lbs after starting with the one-week juice detox. So where these TV docs get their information and research from I am unsure. They simply go on TV and make seemingly random statements which scare people away from drinking vegetable juice.

You would think with the current obesity crisis and the increase in all lifestyle diseases doctors would encourage *anything* that may help even just one person improve their health and drop a few pounds. You would think that with the annual cost to the NHS of over £5 BILLION for obesity-related disease they would look at every option which could help. You would think, given the incredible successes hundreds of thousands of people are reporting all over the world, they would be prescribing fresh juice detox diets in GPs' surgeries, but alas not. I think we are a long way from juicing being recognized as a safe and effective way to lose weight and restore health. It seems just a tad ironic, or rather mind-blowingly insane, that while they are discouraging my juice diets by claiming they are 'crazy' and 'potentially dangerous', they don't mind giving gastric surgery, seemingly to anyone, including children as young as two!

Yes, the youngest ever gastric patient had 70 per cent of his stomach cut out in a bid to help him lose weight after 'diets failed'. How 'crazy' or 'potentially' dangerous is that? How can a diet not work for a two-year-old? Don't you just stop feeding him rubbish? Who the hell is feeding this kid and why aren't we looking at that rather than thinking there's something wrong with the digestive system of the kid? If I had a two-year-old who weighed 5st (70lbs) and was given the choice between feeding him freshly extracted fruit and vegetable juices until he was looking like a normal two-year-old, or putting him under anaesthetic and removing 70 per cent of his stomach, I know which one I would choose. What about you? Seriously, how have we reached a stage where many in the medical profession shout 'danger' about freshly extracted juice, yet, some shout 'good idea' when cutting out 70 per cent of a two-year-old's stomach? If I put a two-year-old on a juice diet and it dissolved 70 per cent of his stomach, I would be locked up!

The argument that 'when they start to eat normally again they'll gain the weight back and more' has one fundamental flaw. To understand this, all we need to do is look at the word 'normally'; it all comes to down to what their idea of *normal* is. If *normally* they eat loads of refined fat, salt and sugar, snack all day long and do no exercise, then yes they will indeed gain weight when they finish the juice detox. This isn't because they just did the juice detox, but because they are overeating rubbish! Wasn't it their 'normal' eating which got them to the stage where they needed to lose weight in the first place? If they go back to their idea of normal then clearly they will simply pick up where they left off and gain weight again, and continue to do so as long as they eat in that way, as that was the direction they were heading in. What they need to do is change their idea of 'normal', which is what this book addresses in the Low H.I Way of Life chapter coming later.

TIME TO OBSERVE

Many dieticians and doctors even go as far as to say you won't lose any weight at all on a juice detox because of all the sugars. I have yet to see anyone who needs to lose weight not do so when they follow this programme to the letter.

A recent article in the UK's *Observer Magazine* highlighted that Gwyneth Paltrow lasted only ten days on a juice cleanse before 'she started hallucinating'. I have been juicing and dealing with thousands of people who are juicing for years and years and I have never, and I mean *never, ever,* heard of anyone hallucinating because of juicing. This article decided to highlight what one woman said happened to her while she was on a juice cleanse, ignoring the millions who have incredible success. It's also important to remember that this article did not confirm what juicing diet Gwyneth was on. There are other approaches to juicing – the famous Lemon Juice diet, for example (also known as the Maple Syrup Diet), which I do not advocate (and is very different to my programmes).

But, specifics aside, in this article, the dietician in question was keen to point out she's not a fan of juice cleansing:

> Like most restrictive diets which cut out a lot of food groups, they can have adverse implications to overall health.

Like what? Gwyneth and her alleged hallucinating aside, exactly what adverse implications to overall health are there? And, while I am here, what food groups are we missing exactly?

During the five-day detox you will be getting amino acids (the building blocks for protein), natural sugars (carbohydrate), essential fatty acids (good fats), vitamins, minerals, water and enzymes. What exactly is missing? Even if you do feel something is missing, it's just five days and you won't become deficient in anything in just five days on this programme.

The dietician also added:

> There is no good scientific evidence that shows a detox
> juice diet is helpful to losing weight.

I had to read and re-read that comment, as I cannot quite believe it. It's this type of nonsense comment that prevents some from trying nature's finest juices as a safe way to lose weight and treat/prevent some lifestyle diseases. There is also no good *scientific evidence* that if you cut someone's legs off they wouldn't be able to walk either. Why? Because who in their right mind would spend money on such science to try and prove such things? It's painfully obvious that if you cut someone's legs off they would no longer be able to walk, in the same way that it's painfully obvious if anyone who is overweight drinks nothing but freshly extracted juice for a week they will lose weight.

I am unsure if there is any actual scientific evidence that shows a 'detox juice diet to be helpful to losing weight', but who in their right mind would spend money trying to obtain such scientific evidence anyway? I can take anyone who is overweight and put them on a freshly extracted juice detox and they will all lose weight – guaranteed! I'm more than happy to be challenged on this at any point by anyone.

As already mentioned, I have received tens of thousands of letters, emails and video diaries which all illustrate this. If you cut out all of the things that make someone fat and put them on freshly extracted fruit and vegetable juices, they will, of course, lose weight. If they don't go back to the crap, and eat healthily after they finish the detox, they also won't gain it back.

Wow! What a phenomenal week in so many aspects. Not only did I feel great in my body (wasn't hungry once!) but my mind was so much clearer! I lost 2.5kgs which is just over 5lbs! ... My body shifted this week, my work shifted, my attitude shifted ...

Lisa Steingold

I did the detox [a few months ago] and loved it so much that I now have one juice meal a day. **I have heaps of energy, my skin and hair look great, and I fit into all my skinny clothes again.** Best thing I ever did. So to all those people who say detox doesn't work. Bah humbug to you!

Anne

But, the dietician quoted in the *Observer Magazine* is not the only one to claim juice diets cause 'adverse implications to overall health'; there was an article in the *Daily Mail* entitled:

JUICING CAN WRECK YOUR LOOKS:
FLAKING SKIN, HAIR LOSS AND ROTTING TEETH.
THE LATEST A-LIST DIET CRAZE HAS SOME UGLY SIDE-EFFECTS

(No I'm not joking, that was a genuine headline in a UK national newspaper). In this article, a spokesperson for the British Dietetic Association was quoted as saying:

Juice fasts are simply not sustainable, so if you're doing it for health reasons, there's simply no point ...

To say a 'juice fast is not sustainable' is to not understand the nature of juice detoxes at all. Firstly, a juice detox is not a 'fast'. A fast is defined by the absence of all food (or nutrition), so to describe a diet consisting of freshly extracted juice as a fast is one illustration of the lack of understanding in this area.

I am also unsure what she means by 'not sustainable'. Nowhere in any of my books do I ever advise people to live on nothing but juice for the rest of their lives. The juice detoxes last short periods of time and are simply designed as a health reboot or a service for your body. They give the body a chance to heal, clear the bloodstream of addictive substances, and act as a springboard to a healthier life.

Having said that, a well-thought-through juice programme is in fact extremely sustainable, for very long periods of time and, it could be argued, for life. I don't advocate anyone lives on nothing but juice for the rest of their lives (you'd be bored out of your skull and have no friends, if nothing else!) but I'd rather someone drink *green blends* (vegetable juices with blended avocado) for life than consume white bread, cheese, crisps, pizzas, burgers and cola! I have seen people live on freshly extracted juices and green blends for months on end with no adverse effects to their health whatsoever. I am writing this having just returned from filming my *Super Juice Me!* documentary, where everyone (including me) lived on nothing but juices and blends for a whole month. And I can tell you now, the results of those who did are out of the park; I genuinely feel incredible on the back of it. A well-thought-out juice detox, which includes green blends and vegetable juices, *is* sustainable for very long periods of time, *but* we are only talking about five days here! Not only is that sustainable, it's what's known as a no brainer.

The dietician then continues ...

> You might be getting a quick sugar rush but you're not consuming any carbohydrates, so exercising, or even normal daily life, is going to be almost impossible. You'll feel light-headed and exhausted.

First up, what does she mean 'no carbohydrates'? *All* fruits and vegetables are carbohydrates! The juice that is squeezed from the fibres (and the only part which actually feeds the body) is loaded with carbon, hydrogen and oxygen, in other words *carbohydrates*. As for the comment about exercising, well, one word: BS! At our retreats, where no solid food is served at all, the average person does about 3–4 hours of exercise every day and leaves the retreat bouncing off the walls. I have run the New York and London Marathons on *nothing* but juice. It is true that during the first 72 hours *some* people (not all by any means) can start to feel an energy low. However this is not caused by juicing, but rather by the withdrawal from refined carbs, refined fats and caffeine. It's a similar energy low some people feel when they stop smoking, where clearly the slump is caused by withdrawal, not a genuine nutritional need for nicotine.

But our state-registered dietician didn't stop there ...

> With no fibre in your diet, even after a couple of days, constipation will become a problem, and in the long term, your cholesterol levels could be affected as fibre

helps keep them low. So, if you're not getting enough fibre, your cholesterol could shoot up.

I've already covered the fibre point, but to say a freshly extracted juice diet could cause cholesterol problems is again a clear illustration of the lack of genuine research in this area. I receive more emails about how juicing helps cholesterol than almost anything else. I think I'll let just a couple of examples speak for themselves:

> I think it's a miracle to change from pre-diabetes to normal sugar levels in 8 days and lower cholesterol too. My cholesterol went from 7.5 to 5.4 in just over one week with juicing.
>
> *Jane B*

> Amazed that my cholesterol has gone down rapidly from 8.2 to 5.0 in just one week!
>
> *Mary L*

Once again, I don't just have one or two of these, I have hundreds. But the dietician quoted in the *Daily Mail* didn't finish there either:

> Vitamin C is, of course, good for you, but beyond a certain point, more isn't any better for you. And, if you're only drinking veg and fruit juices, you're missing out on a lot of other nutrients such as calcium, protein, vitamin D, essential fats and so on.

Seriously? So there's no calcium in oranges, broccoli, kelp, spinach and celery? No protein? No essential fats? Once again, the largest land animals with the biggest muscles are mainly vegan, all gaining their protein, calcium, essential fats and other nutrients from plant foods! It is true that you won't be getting vitamin D, but unless you are locking yourself in your house away from all sunlight for the rest of your life, you'll be OK!

Then the *Daily Mail* called on other experts – a trichologist and a dermatologist – both claiming that juice diets cause adverse effects. Firstly, the experts claimed it can cause hair loss:

> I've seen it many, many times. Women come to see me with what appears to be unexplained hair loss, and then, when you trace it back, it turns out that they were on some extreme juice fast a few months before. It's quite simple, if your body isn't getting the nutrition it needs, it powers down the processes that it considers as being not essential to life, and one of those is hair production.

So, a few months before their hair fell out, they did some juicing; what more proof do you want? Well, if you are a scientist – plenty! How can you possibly equate one with the other? This year Gail Porter came to my retreat. Gail is a well-known presenter who was catapulted into notoriety when a UK magazine beamed her naked image (from the back) onto the Houses of Parliament and Big Ben. The magazine got into a lot of trouble, but it put them, and indeed Gail, on the map. A few years later Gail started to suffer from extreme alopecia and lost all of her hair, including her eyebrows. This she documented in depth in her wonderful autobiography. Within 10 days on my retreat, consuming nothing but freshly extracted juices and blends, some of her hair started to grow back. There was hair on her head and she had eyebrows again for the first time in ten years! I am not saying this is some kind of cure for alopecia, but you cannot say a juice detox diet causes hair to fall out; makes part of a great headline though.

Then it was the turn of the dermatologist:

> Juicing for anything longer than a couple of days will have a profound effect on your skin … if you've already got a tendency to dry skin anyway, you may find that you start to develop patches of eczema …

As you now know, I used to suffer from psoriasis and eczema; I saw lots of dermatologists over the years, none of whom helped. For me, both cleared when I started juicing. This clearly is personal and it isn't a cure for everyone, nor am I suggesting it is, but, once again, I have seen many people who have had incredible benefits to their skin using natural juice therapy. Here are just two examples from hundreds I have received:

> Thanks for my new juicy life! As a result my weight is melting off & my eczema (which I had on my hands & feet & needed steroid cream for) has disappeared.
>
> *Anna*

I have been following the juice plan for a week now and did have very bad dermatitis on my hands and feet and very bad dry skin. Within a week it has literally disappeared! I cannot praise you enough Jason; thank you for changing my long-suffering life.

Dee

THERE ARE SIMPLY NO LOGICAL ARGUMENTS WHATSOEVER!

When you start to look at this with logical common sense, it becomes painfully obvious that no harm will come to you when you live on nothing but freshly extracted juice for just five days. It's simply like putting yourself in for a service, as you would a car. What is crazy is not the fact that people do the juice detox diet, but the fact I am having to write so many pages breaking down the arguments against it. There simply are no rational arguments against this programme, but because of the attacks you will almost certainly receive when you start it, I wanted to cover it all here so you are well armed.

I can guarantee you that once you even voice that you will be living on nothing but juice for five days the arguments will start. It's a strange world we live in, but say to anyone that you will be sticking two fingers up to healthy eating for a week, living on burgers, fries and getting drunk, and the reaction tends to be, 'Good for you, life's too short.' However, tell them you're cutting out all the rubbish from your diet and that you'll be living on nature's finest, freshly extracted juice for a week and get ready to go head-to-head.

Now we need to understand that part of this is often due to their own fear of you getting thin and looking amazing; after all no one wants a hot, thin friend! OK, I'm being a little jovial, but there is more than an element of truth in that statement. What I mean is, simply voicing that you are about to jump on the road to the land of the thin and healthy can highlight that they are not. This often creates an unconscious fear, which in turn causes the friend to attack what you are doing so you will stay on the same road as them. Obviously this isn't always the case and at times the attacks are born out of a genuine concern based on the scaremongering fallacies they have read. But hopefully by the time you start with the programme you will either brush aside any attacks, as you know the truth, or you will be armed with enough knowledge to counter any such arguments.

Part 2

IT'S ALL IN THE MIND

ONWARDS AND UPWARDS!

Right – now the main arguments are out the way, we are almost ready to crack on. However, before you dive in, I want to make sure you don't simply white-knuckle it, but enjoy the process. Many are convinced that a detox of this nature is not something you can ever enjoy, but rather something you grit your teeth through in order to get the result you want. However, the difference between finding this incredibly easy or driving yourself cuckoo for five days is simply a case of …

Mind

OVER

FATTER!

7

A fly is stuck in a room and desperate to get out. A window is open at the top with a clear, easy and obvious escape route. The fly shoots over and flies directly into the *closed* part of the window. The fly, not being the sharpest tool in the box, flies back and prepares itself for another attempt, then once again bangs its head directly into the glass. You would think the fly would stop there, but as you've no doubt witnessed many times yourself, it simply continues to try and escape using exactly the same approach. It just keeps flying into the window, even though there is a very easy way out.

THE POSITIVE THINKING FLY

But what if you persuaded the fly to nip off to a 'positive thinking fly seminar' in order to help it achieve its goal? Imagine if the fly was told at the seminar that it could achieve *anything* if it just had enough determination and positivity. What if the fly also did a 'Fire Walk' at the seminar and came out more positive and determined than it had ever been in its life? What if it was so pumped, so determined, so confident, so positive that it felt anything really was possible – would that attitude do anything to help the fly find the gap at the top of the window? The answer is no. No matter how positive, pumped or determined the fly is physics alone will never allow it to break through the glass!

Many people believe that being positive and focused is the Holy Grail to achieving one's goals, but, although these are great tools, they are often about as useful as an open-topped car in a safari park. The fly can positively bang its head against the glass till the cows come home, but it will never get out of the room while it continues to do this. What the fly needs to do is relax, take a step back (metaphorically speaking, clearly) and open its eyes to the fact there is a different way, an easy way! The fly doesn't need positive thinking; it just needs a change in thinking.

THERE'S ALWAYS ANOTHER WAY!

It's the same with changing your diet, or going on a programme of this nature with a view to ultimately changing your diet. You can make this detox as easy or as difficult as you choose. Unlike the fly, a dash of positive thinking, determination and being a little 'pumped' won't go amiss here, but these thinking tools alone will not make it easy for you. After all, many people kick off a diet with loads of positivity and determination, only to find themselves saying things like, 'life's too short', 'sod this for a game of soldiers' and 'where's the sub?' at lunchtime *on Day 1!* Within no time at all they are driving themselves mad, white-knuckling it, and are just a few hours away from a little binge. Why? Because, like the fly, positive thinking and determination aren't enough; we need to relax, step back and realize there's another way of thinking that can make all the difference.

There are two things here. One is perspective, which I will come to in a second, and that alone can make all the difference you need. The other is a tiny shift in thinking, which is equivalent to seeing the window open.

I Want It but I Can't Have It
I Can Have It but I Don't Want It

One of the biggest mistakes people make when jumping on any detox or diet is falsely believing they can no longer have certain foods or drinks. You may think this is true, especially with something like this juice detox, as there is no solid food whatsoever on the programme, but the truth is you can in fact have whatever you like. I fully realize that sounds like an instant contradiction, but hear me out.

There is nothing, in reality, preventing you from having *anything* you want from Day 1 of starting the detox. You can, after all, keep the fruit and veg in the fridge, leave your juicer as clean as a whistle and tuck into a sandwich and crisps instead. You can even order a pizza, drink loads of fizzy drinks, stuff your face with chocolate and down a bottle or two of wine if you want to. And that indeed is the point here; you don't want to, that's why you are reading this book. You have bought it and will be getting all the fruit and veg and getting your juicer ready because you *want* to do the detox. You *want* to lose weight, you *want* to feel amazing and you *want* this to be a springboard to a healthy life so you can go on feeling amazing and get 'that' body. You don't want to eat the crap and fail, so don't make it hard for yourself by telling your brain you do want to eat it. We are simply looking to make one very simple shift from the usual diet mentality of, 'I want it but I can't have it' to 'I can have it but I don't want it.' That one shift alone can change your world and make it far easier than you ever imagined it could be.

SELF-IMPOSED MENTAL TANTRUM

Whether you find this detox easy or a nightmare is all down to the way *you* think. It's all about what *you* say to yourself. It is not because of a lack of nutrients or not being genuinely fed, because that's not an issue on this plan, it's *purely* down to what you say to yourself and how you think.

Back in the day I used to eat a lot of chocolate, but at times I would go for a few days without it, not because I was on a diet, but because I just didn't feel like eating any. I didn't make a conscious plan to be without chocolate for a few days; it just happened. Did it bother me not having the chocolate? No. Was I using positive thinking, determination and willpower not to have it? Again, no. Did I suffer any withdrawal or go into a tantrum? No. And no doubt there will have been copious amounts of times when you have gone days, and sometimes even a week or so, without certain foods and drinks and it hasn't bothered you one jot. Yet the very second you consciously 'go on a diet' you want them almost immediately and start using willpower, discipline and control and putting yourself into a mini internal mental tantrum. Nothing has changed *physically* between the two situations, it's just in the latter you are just making the same classic mistake 99.99 per cent of people make when going on any kind of detox or diet; you start telling yourself you *can't* have certain things you feel you want, force yourself into what amounts to a self-imposed mental tantrum and start moping around for foods and drinks, which ironically you hope you won't have! And people wonder why they struggle.

MOPING AROUND FOR FOODS AND DRINKS YOU HOPE YOU WON'T HAVE

This is the most insane part of what people do to themselves when on a diet of any kind – they start moping around for foods and drinks which they hope they won't have. If you don't do that you'll find it easy – if you do, you won't. If you start telling yourself you *can't* have this or that you will struggle like crazy. If you know you *can* have whatever you want but are *choosing* not to for five days, you won't.

I am aware this sounds ridiculously simple, but the real question should be: why should anyone find it difficult to live on juice for just five days? I mean it would hardly make a compelling documentary, would it? It's hardly the biggest test of human endurance there's ever been. Yes you will be withdrawing from things like caffeine, refined sugars and so on, but what does this really add up to? Yes you may well feel a little more tired over the first 72 hours as your body learns to run on natural energy, not false stimulants, but so what? Hardly genuinely challenging.

As for the actual withdrawal from these foods and drinks, in real terms these amount to a slight empty insecure feeling every now and then, but there is no physical pain. The slight withdrawal pangs (if you want to call them that) trigger a thought in the mind, 'I want ...' (fill in with whatever food or drink pops in your head). The person with a diet mentality then usually says to themselves, 'I'd love that right now but I *can't* have it', and a feeling of deprivation sets in. It is only this feeling of deprivation that causes the problem. This then triggers an immediate mental tug-of-war and a situation where the person starts to mope around for foods and drinks which they hope they won't have. The withdrawal pangs trigger false hungers; these false hungers subside very quickly and are easy to deal with, providing you recognize what's going on. You don't want the crap, that's why you are doing this! It's a false message created by the withdrawal from refined sugars and it's often the *only* reason why people struggle on any diet. They simply don't know it's false hunger based on withdrawal and so immediately start to fall into the common and ultimately failure-triggering 'CAN'T' syndrome – **C**onstant **A**nd **N**ever-ending **T**antrum. They then try to use their willpower, discipline and determination to resist whatever it is they think they want in that moment and a big internal mental battle begins. This is the same as the fly banging its head against the glass instead of changing its approach and seeing there is in fact an easy way.

Just Shut Up!

For years I have been advising one simple tool that, if used properly, will immediately stop any internal battle and leave you free to enjoy the detox journey: just shut up! If you are in a mental tug-of-war and your head is filled with, say, 'I WANT CHOCOLATE' (for example), then my advice is simple. Either have the chocolate and shut up or don't have it and shut up, but shut up! Sounds harsh, I know, but trust me on this one: it is only the moping around for something you hope you won't have that can possibly cause you any problems. There is a wonderful sketch from Bob Newhart called 'Stop It' which illustrates perhaps the best therapy in the world. If you are ever struggling during the five days because of what *you* are saying to yourself, go to YouTube, type in 'Bob Newhart Stop It' and follow his instructions – it's genius!

IF I DIDN'T KNOW HOW MUCH FOOD I'D ACTUALLY EATEN, HOW HUNGRY WOULD I GENUINELY BE?

Another wonderful tool is to ask yourself this simple question: 'If I didn't know how much food I'd actually eaten, how hungry would I genuinely be?' Most of the time you won't actually be genuinely hungry, but you will convince yourself you are because you work out how long it's been since you've had any food. Firstly, on this programme you are getting food, it's just no longer in a solid form. Every cell in your body is being fed, so don't try to convince yourself you aren't being fed, because you are. Secondly, ask yourself on a scale of one to ten, *on a physical level*: how hungry are you really? If you aren't in physical pain and feel all uptight and anxious, that's not a lack of nutrients, but rather the withdrawal from refined fats and sugars; it's the false mental hunger I was talking about. If or when these moments happen, some people find it helps to envisage a 'junk food terrorist' who was controlling their life. Every time they feel it asking to be fed, they get real joy in telling it, in no uncertain terms, where to go and letting it starve to death!

If that approach doesn't cut it for you, as it's sometimes too simplistic for some to get their head around, then maybe a little perspective is all that's needed.

JUST KEEP SWIMMING

On Monday 5 September 2011 the famous comedian David Walliams set out for a little swim up the Thames to raise money for charity. Eight days and 140 miles later, he finished his 'little' swim. To put this in perspective, when people swim the channel, depending on the route, it's about 21 miles. David swam the equivalent of *seven* channel crossings in just eight days. He would swim for 11–12 hours some days and hit many obstacles along the way, none more so than 'Thames Tummy'. On Day 2 torrential rain had forced Thames Water to dump 500,000 cubic metres of sewage into the very waters David would be swimming through. 'We're not public health experts, but I wouldn't recommend swimming in it,' said Thames Water's Richard Aylard.

Swallowing Thames water – with the attendant risks of contracting *E. coli*, salmonella and hepatitis – is not desirable but proved unavoidable for David. Despite getting *extremely* ill, he just kept swimming. Despite hurting beyond belief as the true enormity of what he had taken on took its toll each day, he just kept swimming. Despite battling with delusional and paranoid thoughts as he was left with his own company for hours and hours each day, he just kept swimming. At his lowest points, he focused on why he was doing it. He would conjure up the image of a 12-year-old orphan, called Philip, whom he met living in a centre in Kenya funded by Sport Relief, and who wanted to be a pilot. 'He's living in the most desperate circumstances, yet he still has great aspirations,' he said. 'I think about him and not wanting to let him down.' In the end David raised over £1 million for charity and what he did was worthy of world news and a documentary.

The reason I mention his story is to put into total perspective what you will be doing. I have had people say to me, 'I know this is going to be one of the hardest weeks of my life.' To which I always reply, 'Can we swap lives please?' All you are doing is drinking freshly extracted juice for just five days and doing a bit of exercise, hardly a superhuman feat of endurance; hardly worthy of headline news. You are also doing this because *you* want to. You are doing this so that *you* feel thinner, healthier and so you can get rid of some (or all) of any addictions to certain foods or drinks. You are doing this so that *you* feel recharged and in order to get *your* mojo back. I am not undermining your efforts, but it's not exactly in the same league as swimming the 140-mile long River Thames! Just think, when you finish, David would still be swimming. It was *eight* days, 11–12 hours a day in the water. You are simply living on juice for five days; you aren't changing anything else in your life except what you put into your mouth. There is no reason on earth why this should be difficult or why you shouldn't easily complete it, and indeed go on to achieve whatever health or body goal you want.

The good news is that because the vast majority of people do in fact think that a juice detox is something that's amazingly difficult, they'll all think you're amazing. They will think you are even more incredible when you aren't struggling, but actually enjoying the process. It will drive some of them mad too. After all no one minds you getting thin and healthy as long as you're miserable about it (gives them hope you'll fail), but start whistling and smiling through the process and they often hate you!

However, because it's the norm for people to put themselves into a self-imposed mental tantrum, use willpower, discipline, suffer the 'CAN'T' syndrome and effectively be the fly, people around you will start thinking you are superhuman when you are actually enjoying the process. The strangest thing is, you'll feel superhuman yourself too!

Remember, the *only* reason why people struggle is because they *feel* they are making a sacrifice. Yet all the sacrifices are made when you *are* eating the rubbish. You sacrifice your health, your energy and so many other aspects of your life. It's not often talked about, but just not being able to wear what you want can affect a large part of your daily life. Hating the way you look and feel can affect a person for the vast majority of their day, *every day*. Not having the pure raw energy to really suck the juice out of life can get to a person, *every day*.

This is why I have added this small chapter into the book – I genuinely care if you do this programme. I could have easily just written the plan and left out all the other stuff, but if *anything* in this book helps just one more extra person lift themselves from the hazy fog of rubbish foods and drinks, then it's worth adding it in. These 'Mind Over Fatter' techniques may seem ridiculously simple, but that's because they are, and if you follow them it makes the detox itself ridiculously simple too!

IN THE ABSENCE OF EXCUSES ANYTHING IS POSSIBLE!

There is only one thing in reality that prevents people from getting the body and health they ultimately crave, or doing a programme of this nature – excuses. I have come to the conclusion that there are two types of people in this world: people who *do* and people who *talk*. The people who do, simply crack on with it; the people who talk, simply talk about doing it *one day* while coming up with excuse after excuse as to why they can't at this particular time.

Someday is not a day of the week!

The people who talk start each sentence with: 'I would love to do that, but I can't now because ...', and will finish the sentence with whatever they see fit. The amount of people I know who say, 'I would get thin and healthy, *but ...*' is a joke. I call it 'The But Syndrome' and you may have suffered with it on many occasions yourself: 'but I can't because of this or that'. It's this simple:

The More Buts You Have
the Bigger Butt You're Likely to Have!

Just stop the excuses, use the Mind Over Fatter tools, put this five-day juice detox into total perspective, ignore the uneducated juice sceptics and the body and health you crave are there for the taking! Everything you need is laid out in the following pages. Make sure you read each section and then pick the book up again on Day 5 to read 'The Rough After Plan' (pp. 191–197), 'The Low-H.I Way of Life' (pp. 199–209), 'The Law of Four' (pp. 211–216) and 'Be Limitless and Make Your Life Extraordinary' (pp. 217–226) chapters at the end of this book. They make all the difference between this being a quick five-day detox and a springboard for a massive life change. Not many books ask you to come back on a certain day, but you will be feeling very different on Day 5 and will be better placed to tap into the information in that part of the book. It explains what to do after the programme. You are more than welcome to read it before you start too, as many have said that was beneficial. But if you do read it now, please also make a point of coming back on Day 5 and re-reading it then.

IT WILL ALSO HELP TO SEE A DOC BEFORE YOU START

No, not a doctor; a documentary. There seems to be a massive increase in health documentaries taking the world by storm. Morgan Spurlock kicked things off years ago with *Super Size Me*. He ate nothing but McDonald's for a month to see what would happen. Since then there have been many documentaries in this genre exposing the food industry and inspiring people to make a change. Some are better than others, but you are looking for any tools during these five days to make it easier for yourself, I am a strong believer that your life is a direct result of what you feed yourself, and I don't just mean what you put into your mouth. I am also talking about what you feed your eyes, your ears and your soul. While you are ridding your body of junk, I also encourage you to get rid of the junk coming into your eyes and ears at the same time. Read as much, and watch as much, on this subject as you can over the five days; it really can make a massive difference. Currently I would recommend: *Hungry for Change, Food Matters* and *Super Juice Me!*. It's not as if you won't have the time; you're not cooking, after all!

Right – if you are like most people, you'll be itching to start now. But remember: if you fail to prepare you prepare to fail. With that in mind, here are your …

TOP TEN
TIPS FOR
JUICY
SUCCESS

8

I. MAKE IT EASY FOR YOURSELF!

You will notice that each day, although there are four juices, there are just two different types. Your morning and evening juices are exactly the same, as are your lunch and late afternoon juices. The reason I have designed the plan like this is to make it extremely easy to follow, while ensuring your nutritional needs are met. Although I am a big advocate of drinking juices within 30 minutes of making them fresh, I am also a realist. Many people just don't have the time to make a fresh juice four times a day and this can often mean they fall at the first hurdle. With this in mind, here are my suggestions of how to make it easy for yourself. Either:

A **Make all the juices in the morning, store them in cold flasks and then drink throughout the day. As there are only two different juices a day it means you only have to make a double batch of each juice and you're done!**

If you are doing it this way, it is important to make and store the juice as quickly as possible. You are trying to prevent too much oxygen and light getting to the juice, as this can cause it to oxidize and in turn lose vital nutrients. Use a good thermos flask to store (SIGG brand, for example).

B **Make and drink juice number 1 when it's 100 per cent fresh, make and store juices 2 and 3 in advance (as above), then make your fourth 'dinner' juice fresh at home.**

The reason for this is three-fold:

1 The longer you leave any juice, even in a flask, you will lose nutrients, so by having your first and fourth juices made fresh you are getting those ones 100 per cent fresh still, which is always best where possible.

2 It's good for the mind to be in the kitchen making something for 'dinner', even if it's not what you usually have. And it means that if you have a family, and there's action in the kitchen, you aren't left out.

3 You only need to clean your juicer twice a day!

This is the option I would highly encourage (based on 15 years of juice detox experience), as I feel it's a nice halfway house between 100 per cent fresh and the convenience of pre-prepared. Feel free to make all juices fresh at the time of drinking them (that's the ideal, but I realize it is not realistic for most).

C **If you really hate the thought of having to juice every day, you can even make all the juices on one day, store them in a bunch of BPA-free water bottles and freeze them. Then simply move your juices for the next day to the fridge each night and bingo, you're done.**

The potential issue with this is you lose some nutrients (not huge amounts as freezing retains around 95 per cent of nutrients) and also the juice can taste a little 'flat'. But it's an option, and I know it's easiest for some people, and it's better than not doing it at all where you clearly lose 100 per cent of the nutrients!

D The final option, and one more and more people are taking up due to time pressures, is to have all your juices delivered directly to your door.

This service is available at www.juicemasterdelivered.com. We juice everything in twin gear masticating (slow) juicers or hydraulic presses, and immediately lock in the high-quality nutrients by blast freezing them. We then deliver the juice, still frozen, direct to your door. You then just take the juice out the night before, place it in the fridge and drink at the appropriate time the next day. You don't lose a great deal of the nutrients when you freeze the juice and, as they are made in the finest slow juicers, the quality of the juice – even once frozen – is often higher than if you made it fresh at home with a fast speed juicer.

Having said that, I am still a massive advocate of juicing 100 per cent fresh wherever you can and this service is only intended for those who really don't have time to shop, prepare, juice and clean the juicer! If you can juice at home then put down the lazy brush and get juicing.

2. GET THE RIGHT JUICER!

Nothing will put a nail in your juicing coffin faster than picking the wrong juicer. There are all kinds of juicers on the market and the best juicer is the one that's right for you and your needs. For the record, a NutriBullet-type machine is *not* a juicer – it's a blender. For this plan you will need both a juicer *and* a blender, but don't confuse one with the other. Please go to page 255 and read Chapter 20, **So Which Juicer Is Best, Jase?**, so you have a clear understanding of the range of juicers and blenders on the market and the differences between them.

3. HUNGER SOS!

At some point during the 5-day juice plan you may well have a couple of **I NEED FOOD!** moments. These will mainly be mental hungers, and not a genuine physical hunger, as your body will be being fed the pure bio-available nutrition it needs. However, they do feel very real and at these times you may need to use your SOS card.

Once a day you can eat an emergency avocado, banana, small handful of berries or a good natural food bar, like Juice in a Bar or the Simply Nude range of raw energy bars. Personally, I would always choose either an avocado or veggie Juice in a Bar, but these are my personal choices and you may want something else. A nice ripe avocado with lemon juice and some cracked black pepper really hits the spot; it's the most nutritious fruit on the planet and the good fats help to curb any hunger within 5 to 15 minutes.

The other thing that hits the mark beautifully, especially during the evenings, is a veggie Juice in a Bar and a large mug of peppermint tea with a small teaspoon of Manuka honey. In fact, for many, this Hunger SOS is their saving grace and can be the difference between success and failure. I really look forward to this in the evenings and every time I have done this particular plan, on about three days of the five, I always have my veggie bar and pep tea in the evening. It more than takes the edge off and really satisfies. I spent over a year developing what I believe to be the most nutritious and natural energy bar on the market today. It also won *Best New Food Product of the Year* award at the Natural & Organic Trade Show in London.

Clearly there are many other perfectly good raw energy bars on the market, so please shop around, and have any that float your boat with your evening herbal tea. I am biased clearly, but choose your hunger SOS wisely, and make sure it's 100 per cent raw with no added nasties. In other words, don't choose a doughnut!

Important note to all the cheeky ones out there: the SOS card is not transferable to other days! So, if by Friday you haven't had an SOS, don't think you can eat five avocados or five Juice in a Bars that day. Ideally you won't ever use your SOS card; it is there for emergency situations.

4. GET YOUR MIND RIGHT AND THE BODY WILL FOLLOW

Being in the right frame of mind is often the difference between success and failure. To me it's the difference between struggling and finding it easy, and the difference between a *diet mentality* and a *freedom mentality*. There is no reason this has to be difficult at all. It's only five days and you're having wonderful juices packed with all the nutrients you need, plus you have a hunger SOS card to play once a day if you feel like it. I would highly recommend using the simple techniques found in the 'Mind Over Fatter' chapter and, if you can, getting the 5lbs in 5 days app. It has five full days of coaching that can make a fundamental difference to many people. Clearly not everyone will need this coaching and many will feel fired up just by the few inspirational stories at the start of this book, but never underestimate the difference a little support each day can provide.

For those who are used to doing the *7lbs in 7 Days: Super Juice Diet*, it's nice to know that this plan is much easier for many reasons: the way the juices have been devised (just two different juices each day); the fact there are four juices a day, not five; and the fact it's a five-day plan, not a seven-day one, meaning most people can still keep their weekends free. Also, if you follow this plan to the letter, you will lose 7lbs, but in five days, not seven!

As I said, each night I would also *highly* recommend feeding the mind with health documentaries such as *Super Juice Me!*, *Food Matters* and *Hungry for Change*. There are others, but these are the best at this time and will help to get your brain fully engaged with this change. I'd watch one a night for the first four nights, starting with either *Super Juice Me!* or *Hungry for Change*.

5. EXERCISE YOUR RIGHT TO BE THIN!

I have been running juice and fitness retreats for ten years, and breakfast is always the same – water, followed by exercise, then juice. If you want the maximum results on this programme and want to lose more like 10lbs in five days, rather than 5lbs, make sure you exercise for 30 minutes, twice a day. And when I say exercise, I don't mean walking around the gym talking to your friends and checking your texts and Twitter every two minutes (I've seen you!); I mean working out until you sweat, really sweat.

Please do not make the very common mistake of thinking you need massive amounts of fuel before a 30-minute workout in the morning. If you are doing this to lose weight, trust me, you have enough *fuel* in storage to keep you going! It's this very *fuel* you want shot of. The reason for no food before the morning workout is so you get into *fat-burning* and not *sugar-burning* mode. It is also extremely important, if you only have one hour available a day for exercise, to not do the full hour at once. Research has shown doing two separate high-intensity workouts a day will have a longer after-burn effect and will be around *40 per cent more effective* in terms of weight loss than if you did the full hour just in the morning or just in the evening.

Please make sure you read 'Exercise Your Right to Be Thin!' (pp. 125–129) and 'Super After-Burn 30/30' (pp. 131–140) for exactly what to do for maximum rapid fat-burning weight loss.

6. RECHARGE YOUR BODY!

Rest is just as vital as exercise. When you fall into a beautiful deep sleep you are effectively recharging yourself. It's like plugging yourself in overnight in order to power up for the next day. Good sleep is just as important as good nutrition and physical exercise, and yet it's an area many often struggle with. The reason so many of us fail to get a good night's sleep is due to the *false stimulants* we consume daily. Very rarely, if ever, does your body get a full good night's sleep because of this.

I get more emails from people saying their insomnia has vanished or improved than almost anything else. It is this factor, more than the fresh juices, which is behind the surge in genuine energy experienced at the end of the five-day plan.

You may find that during the first three days you are, at times, disproportionately tired. This is down to the *withdrawal* from refined sugars, refined fats, caffeine and the like. This will be gone in 72 hours, after which most people start to experience what is known as the *juice high*. With no false stimulants coming in, the body taps into its own natural energy reserves, meaning your energy is no longer a nervous one, but a natural one.

7. AVOID GOING ALL OCD!

If you are on any prescribed medication always consult your doctor before embarking on any plan of this nature, and obviously do not come off any prescribed drugs unless your GP advises you to. However, if you are an OCD pill popper, my advice would be to *detox* from those too while you are on the plan (and beyond, ideally). What I mean by an *OCD pill popper* is Over-the-Counter Drugs. If you were to pick up the average person walking down the street in the UK and shake them, they would rattle. We almost have OCD about OCDs; that's Obsessive Compulsive Disorder about Over-the-Counter-Drugs. We are popping drugs without questioning what we are doing. We have reached the stage where unconsciously we think a headache is caused by a lack of aspirin or indigestion by a lack of Rennie! ALL drugs are liver toxic and if you want a genuine full five-day clean up stop the OCDs – your bank balance and your body will be better off for it.

We spend almost £600 million on over-the-counter drugs a year in the UK, this adds up to almost ONE BILLION purchases. The global market for over-the-counter drugs is expected to surpass £50 billion ($70 billion) by 2015. According to estimates from the Consumer Healthcare Products Association, retail sales of OCD medicines in the US in 2010 were worth $23 billion. In my opinion, the vast majority of these drugs are being taken totally unnecessarily. Once again though, and I want to make this very clear, if you are taking any drugs, even OCDs, as part of *doctor's orders*, then speak to your doctor before stopping taking them.

8. EVERYONE WANTS A HOTTIE!

The vast majority of people in the UK believe they can't make it through the day without their daily cup of tea or coffee. These are 100 per cent no no's on the 5-Day juice plan, but as I recognize we sometimes need something hot, here's my suggestion.

Peppermint tea (or the like) should become your new best friend over the next five days. If you usually go into Starbucks (other coffee chains are available …) still go, but instead of your usual *milkshake and sugar with a little added coffee* (which, let's face it, is what the vast majority of people order), have a peppermint tea. The trick is to go for the large size (or Vente as they call it; *large* would be just too simple!), ask for two teabags, leave them in and ask for a few ice cubes (as they serve it while it's still boiling!). You can even, if you must, have a little honey for sweetness. Who knows, in five days, you may not even bother to go back to coffee or normal tea, as,

A it actually tastes good;

B it's light and refreshing and 100 per cent calorie free; and

C it's so much cheaper than a latte!

So if you fancy a little *hottie* to help yourself through the five days, try herbal or fruit tea.

9. GO ORGANIC WHERE POSSIBLE!

It's only five days and the juices are all you are having, so if you are going to do it and you have the money then do it right! I am fully aware organic can be more expensive, and it's the first thing people usually say. However, think about it. You won't be having anything else for five days, so even if you go all organic, it will still be cheaper for most people than what they usually spend in a five-day period on takeaways, snacks, alcohol, soft drinks, meals out and chocolate … the list goes on. Just a meal out for two sets you back an average of £50–£80, if you include wine, and the average total cost of organic produce for this five-day programme is about £100.

Clearly, it's almost impossible to get everything organic for this plan, but most supermarkets now do organic apples and carrots, and, these days, usually at the same price as non-organic. As many of the juice bases contain apple, it's worth at least using organic apples even if you cannot get hold of anything else.

There are two main reasons for going organic:

1 Studies have shown that organic produce contains 40 per cent more nutrition than non-organic on average.

2 You won't be ingesting the often-harmful pesticides, herbicides and fungicides.

If you really can't get hold of, or afford, organic, do not despair. There are many good local farms which, although not always certified *organic*, use much fewer chemicals than those which supply the mass-market supermarket chains. Although I try to use organic where possible, I am also aware that even *normal* fruits and vegetables still contain a great deal more nutrients than a doughnut! If I'm not using organic I always *Super Supp* myself at the same time (see tip 10).

10. SUPER SUPP YOURSELF!

If you aren't going to use organic produce I would recommend adding some super supplements in the form of Power Greens to your morning and evening juices. These are the *thicker* ones and, as such, the super green powders would be blended. Power Greens are a powder of dried super foods, such as whole leaf barley grass, whole leaf wheatgrass, nettle leaf, alfalfa leaf juice, dandelion leaf juice, barley grass juice, oat grass juice, burdock root, broccoli juice, kale juice, spinach juice, parsley juice, ginger root, spirulina, chlorella and kelp, as well as digestive enzymes and friendly bacteria.

They are a perfect addition to this programme when you aren't sure of the nutritional value of some of the fruits and vegetables you are using. If you are getting everything organic there is no need to use these types of powders, but if you want to raise the game nutritionally, add some super greens. Power Green powders are not like vitamin and mineral tablets: they are dried foods. You might not see this powder as food, but your body very much will. There are many brands on the market, but Juice Master's Power Greens (previously Juice Master's Ultimate Superfood) are very good. I already hear you shouting, *'Yes, but you would say that wouldn't you, as that's your brand.'* There are many other green powders on the market, some very good, so feel free to get any one you wish – just do your research and make sure you are getting the real deal, otherwise it's not worth your time or money. I searched for two years to find the right combination of super green powders and I know just how good ours are.

I would suggest adding a teaspoon to juices 1 and 4 every day (these juices are thicker than juices 2 and 3, so it's easy to blend the powders in). Please do a taste test first though; you may find you love the juices without the powder, and hate them with. If this is the case, leave the powder out and have it separately in water. Just add to a bottle of water, shake it and drink. It's an acquired taste, but as all the juices are so delicious, it's a nice reminder you are on a detox. Sometimes if it's too easy and everything tastes too wonderful, we aren't convinced it's doing us any good!

Part 3

THE 5LBS IN 5 DAYS DETOX PROGRAMME

Exercise *YOUR RIGHT* TO BE THIN!

9

Exercise, like nutrition, is an area where the accepted and proven science seems to change all the time. Should you stretch your muscles before a workout, or after a workout, or both? Well, the answer to that question depends on which year you're asking it in, suggesting once again that science about exercise, like so much of that in the nutrition world, is more of a hypothesis than an established fact. After all, if an established fact is proved to be untrue years later, it was never in reality a fact; it was always just a calculated hunch based on the current thinking at that time. The problem is that the calculated hunch often gets written up as a fact in an established paper such as the *British Medical Journal* and everyone ends up believing it as fact until it's proved otherwise. Confused? So I am most of the time, with the many constant changes in physical fitness dos and don'ts.

What I am not confused about is that the vast majority of people need not be so concerned with whether they stretch before or after a workout, or don't stretch, but with whether they are going to get off their backside and actually move! And no matter how big you are, you can always move something. Kelly Gneiting proved this when he became the heaviest person ever to complete a marathon. Despite being a whopping 400lbs (28 stone 8lbs) in weight, the 6ft tall ex-sumo wrestler finished the marathon in 9 hours 48 minutes and 52 seconds. So if you think you can't move for whatever reason, think of Kelly.

The suggested exercises I have laid out here are designed to create maximum fat burn rate and phenomenal results on the weight-loss front. Some may be asking if the Super After-burn (SAB) exercise programme is scientifically proven? The answer – nope! But is it extremely effective? Yes! And isn't that really all you care about? I'm a firm believer in not getting caught up in trying to analyse why something works, as long as it works. I've seen people studying for years to try and figure out exactly what elements within an apple, for example, affect healing so profoundly – while at the same time eating doughnuts at their desk. They may die prematurely, but at least they know a great deal about an apple! Sometimes you don't have to know how it works, just that it works ... as long as you actually eat it or do it.

You can, of course, do the 5lbs in 5 Days juice programme with no exercise at all and still drop 5lbs in 5 days, doing exactly what it says on the tin. However, when you introduce exercise of this nature into this equation, you start turning months into weeks and the level of weight loss goes up a notch or three. Not only that, but as you stimulate brain chemicals such as dopamine and serotonin (the happy brain chemicals) this type of exercise makes the detox much, much easier on the *happy to do it* rather than *not wanting to kill someone* front – so it's a genuine win/win.

This type of exercise also keeps the metabolism high throughout the week. This is of particular benefit for when you finish the five days on juice only and move onto solid food, as your metabolism can slow down slightly. This doesn't always happen, and all depends on the exercise side of life, but it can happen. So I would highly recommend doing the exercise part of the plan.

Some will say they don't have the time, but it's just for five days, and for as little as 30 minutes in the morning and the same at night. How long do you usually spend making breakfast or dinner? *If you are committed, there's always a way* and the results are just too good not to.

Gone are the days of pounding the treadmill for hours and getting nowhere very slowly. Exercise has gone broadband ... faster speeds get faster results! Welcome to the world of ...

SUPER
AFTER-BURN
30/30
THE RAPID WEIGHT-LOSS EXERCISE PROGRAMME

10

The Super After-burn 30/30 or SAB rapid weight-loss exercise programme is highly effective on its own, but do it while living on fresh juice for five days and you've just taken rapid weight loss to a whole new level. It has now been scientifically proven that if you run at a steady pace for 90 minutes, you'll burn nowhere near as much fat as if you did high-tenacity training for 30 minutes. It has also been shown that when you split your exercise you burn hundreds more calories than if you did it all in one go. For example, a study in *Men's Health* magazine showed that cyclists who did two 25-minute bike sessions burnt 400 calories more than those who did just one 50-minute session.

As soon as you finish a blast of exercise the body continues to burn fat for a period afterwards; this is called 'after-burn'. If you do one 60-minute workout a day you will only get the benefit of one after-burn, whereas if you split the hour into two 30-minute sessions you have the massive benefit of two after-burns. The after-burn effect can last for many hours after the workout, which is why it is more beneficial for weight loss to *split* your exercise into two: one blast in the morning and one in the evening. After-burn turns you into a *fat-burning furnace* for many hours after you have finished your workout. If you then add *high-intensity exercise* into the equation, or broadband exercise as I call it, you combine the two most effective weight-loss exercise tools we have at our disposal today. The beauty of SAB exercise training is the way it combines these two exercise disciplines to give maximum results in the shortest possible time, once again condensing success. It also makes the workout less scary. If you feel you have to run a half marathon, it may cause you to not even start, but 30 minutes – **anyone** can do that.

I could go into the full science of behind this kind of training, but you don't need to spend hours reading about it – you just need to do it. Many people talk a great game, but it's those who go beyond talking and *take consistent action* who ultimately get the results.

I have been involved in health, fitness and nutrition for over 15 years and I can safely say I have never seen such explosive rapid weight-loss results as the combination of the 5lbs in 5 Days Juice Detox Diet and the SAB 30/30 exercise programme. Everyone has their own theories when it comes to exercise, but for the next five days, forget what you have read or what you believe and follow this to the letter and have faith.

Clearly it goes without saying that you should always check with your GP before embarking on any strenuous exercise programme; please also use your intuition and common sense to gauge how you feel during it. And the great news is that SAB 30/30 couldn't be easier:

1. HYDRATE!

On waking, have some hot water and lemon, a nice big peppermint tea (or similar) and/or a large glass of water. If you have some Power Greens then add these to water, shake and have a large glass before exercise. But whatever you drink, drink it slowly; you don't want a stitch!

2. CHOOSE YOUR EXERCISE WEAPON

Whenever I do this programme, I always pick one type of exercise for the whole week, but feel free to pick a different one each day. I like running, and I highly recommend it for this, but SAB exercise works well on any exercise completed on a machine, such as the bike, cross-trainer or rower. For the purposes of this, I will refer to a treadmill, but please adapt accordingly.

3. TWO-MINUTE WARM-UP

Jump on your exercise machine of choice and begin your 2-minute warm-up. This doesn't mean walking pace, it means jogging pace. This is enough to get your heart rate up and get your body ready for the Super Burn.

4. TWENTY-SIX-MINUTE SUPER BURN

This is where you run at a pace that is faster than is usually comfortable. If you take the level of exercise as an effort scale – 1 being the easiest and 10 being the hardest for you – then you want to be running at a level 8.5.

The key behind *high-intensity exercise* is just that – high intensity! You want to run at a level where, if someone were talking to you, it would be difficult to hold a conversation. We are going way beyond the comfortable jog here and moving to exercise where you sweat, really sweat. Jogging tends to be an effort level of about a 5 to 7, but here you need to raise the game and run/skip/bike/row/cross train at an 8.5 level.

I'll give you an example: I usually run at 7.8–8 miles per hour if I am doing an hour or less of running, about 7.5 for anything past that. It is a good pace but its not super-burn rate, for me. I say, for me, as the effort scale is clearly individual. For some people 8 miles an hour is very slow and would only hit a 6 on their exercise effort scale (think of James Cracknell, for example). For others, 8 miles an hour would have their heart popping out of their chest and be a 10+ on their effort scale. So, for me, 8 miles an hour, or 13 kilometres an hour if you prefer, is about a level 7. A good pace and great for a 6-mile run, but as stated it's not a super-burn rate for me. In order to hit an effort level of 8.5, I need to hit 8.5 mile an hour (14.5 kph); then I'm in the super-burn zone. When I run at this pace, I know I have done a workout and I find it hard, which is the idea. For some of you, simply walking very fast may well be your 'super-burn' pace. It's all about how it is for you.

Clearly this is easy to cheat, as it's an individual scale, but you know what level 8.5 means for you and it's only yourself you'll be cheating. Raise the game and raise the results! You want to run at this pace for 26 minutes. But, please be intelligent and if you feel faint then **STOP!** Don't just push through if your body is clearly telling you to stop. You may start on a level 8.5 and it may be too much for you for 26 minutes and you may well need to go at level 8. Your body will tell you if it's genuinely in trouble, but equally you will know if you have just given up. Just use your common sense, but at the same time be wary of throwing in the towel too early. You'll soon get the hang of what level you need to be at.

5. TWO-MINUTE MADNESS!

For the last 2 minutes of the 30 you want to move to level 10 on the exercise effort front. This is where you will feel as if your heart may pop out of your chest. But it's only 2 minutes and will make a fundamental difference to the after-burn effect once you have finished your exercise. Working on my scale above, this would be moving from 8.5 mph to 10mph (or 16kph), or slightly above. That's the speed I'd move to to go flat out for 2 minutes.

THAT'S IT!

Do that twice a day while on the 5lbs in 5 Days Juice Detox Diet and you'll turn 5lbs in 5 days into 10lbs in 5 days easily. You are more than welcome to do additional exercise, if you wish, but please make sure you do the SAB 30/30.

I love my mini-trampoline (or rebounder as they are also known) and I always do at least 20 minutes a day on that. I tend to go on it before I do my SAB 30/30 and I also tend to do some resistance training with some weights after it – it's all down to how much time I have. One thing for sure though: when I'm doing this programme I always make time for at least the SAB 30/30.

The mornings don't tend to be the issue, as you soon get into a routine of getting up and just doing it; it's the evenings where the excuses tend to rear their ugly heads. I know I keep saying it, but I cannot emphasize it enough; the programme is just five days and if you cannot commit to something for just five days when you will be the one getting all of the physical rewards, you have to perhaps start asking serious questions of yourself.

Yes, after a hard day's work it's not always easy, and yes it's easy to seemingly justify why you *can't* do it, but there's always a way if you are committed. The good news is its just 30 minutes and then it's done. You will always be extremely pleased you did it and it actually helps you to unwind, no matter how stressful your day has been. Most people turn to refined sugars, refined fats and highly processed foods, but exercise is the single fastest route out of lethargy and stress and you will never regret doing it. Thirty minutes to make you feel great and proud you followed through on your promise to yourself, or all night beating yourself up for not doing it. It's your call ...

Short-term Pain for Long-term Pleasure
or
Short-term Pleasure for Long-term Pain

Personally, I find it much easier to just do it. The cost of not doing it just lingers all night. Once you have created the pattern of doing the SAB 30/30 and it becomes part of your daily life, it will become a habit. And fundamentally that is my goal for you. Some may decide to do the juice cleanse simply to get into that party dress, but many will be using this as a catalyst to life-long change. This is why it is so important to get habits built daily and to do the programme to the letter.

It is also just as important, if not more so, to be smart after the programme. It's no good living on nothing but nature's finest for five days, and committing to the rapid fat-burning exercise twice a day, if you are going to stuff your face with junk and sit on the sofa the week after. I have mentioned several times how I like to *condense success* and turn months into week, but you need to remember there are limits to what can be achieved in just five days. This detox is meant to be a catalyst to life-long change on the diet and exercise front. I am not suggesting perfection, just a few simple key principles to make sure you don't undo all the good you have just done. With that in mind, when you reach Day 5, please remember to read 'The Rough After Plan' (pp. 191–197), 'The Low H.I. Way of Life' (pp. 199–209), 'The Law of Four' (pp. 211–216) and 'Be Limitless and Make Your Life Extraordinary' (pp. 217–226).

For now, on with the programme ...

THE
STEP-BY-STEP
Guide
TO THE
5-DAY
PLAN

11

YOUR TYPICAL DAY

Your Morning

Step 1: On rising, drink a glass of water (hot or cold) with a squeeze of lemon or lime. If you are using the Power Greens add these to water you drink first thing. You can't beat some hot water and lemon to get things moving.

Step 2: Do 30 minutes of SAB exercise (run, rebound, yoga, bike ride, etc.). If you are going to exercise, do it right – in this case that's until you sweat (sorry, perspire) ... a lot!

Step 3: Drink a large mug of herbal tea (I recommend peppermint tea – Pukka or Tea-Pigs brand if you can, as they taste so good – with a small teaspoon of Manuka active honey, if that takes your fancy).

Step 4: Make your juices (see my recommendations in 'Top Ten Tips for Juicy Success', (pp. 109–122).

Step 5: Between 8 and 10am, drink your daily Ginger Shot (The Healthy Espresso).

Step 6: Again, between 8 and 10am, drink your first juice of the day.

Your Day-time

Step 7: Between 12 and 2pm, drink your second juice of the day.

Step 8: Between 3 and 5pm, drink your third juice of the day.

Go about your day in any way you see fit, remembering to drink your delicious juices on time so your sugar levels don't crash. Otherwise you'll end up eating anything!

Your Evening

Step 1: Do 30 minutes of SAB exercise (time of your choosing, but I'd recommend just after work and before your final juice).

Step 2: Between 7 and 9pm drink your fourth and final delicious (ideally, freshly-made) juice. In an evening emergency, use your HUNGER SOS option. If, a couple of hours after your final juice, you feel stupidly hungry for whatever reason, feel free to use your SOS option.

Step 3: Around 9pm, drink a large mug of herbal tea. I recommend chamomile with a little Manuka honey to help you sleep. Many people also use this time to play their SOS card and have a Juice in a Bar (or Simply Nude bar) with their tea. When I do this plan, I opt for a veggie Juice in a Bar and the biggest cup of herbal tea with a spoonful of Manuka honey. Others opt for an avocado with cracked black pepper and lemon juice.

Step 4: Turn the TV/tablet/phone/PlayStation off and turn on a little relaxation music to help you drift off to sleep. Getting a good night's sleep is a very important part of this programme. Aim for eight hours (before you shout, I said, aim!). Often we sit aimlessly at a screen of some kind for a couple of hours in the evening; why not skip that and use this valuable time to recharge with some good quality sleep.

DAY 1

The times included below are my recommended times, but, as detailed in the step-by-step plan, you can be flexible with these. For example, many people take their ginger shot at the same time as they make their juice and then pop their juices into flasks to have later. If you're up at 6am and making your juices for the day, please feel free to down your ginger shot then if you want. The times below are based on what we have been doing at our health retreats for years, but storing your ginger shot to take later may prove one storage container too many, so please feel free to down it when you please ... even before the SAB training if needed.

9:55am	**Ginger Shot** (The Healthy Espresso)
10am	**Juice 1:** Turbo ... with a Kick!
1pm	**Juice 2:** The Natural Energizer
4pm	**Juice 3:** The Natural Energizer
7pm	**Juice 4:** Turbo ... with a Kick!
Any time	**Herbal Teas** (fresh or tea bags)
Any time	**Hunger SOS** (optional, in case of emergency!)

DAY 2

9:55am	**Ginger Shot** (The Healthy Espresso)
10am	**Juice 1:** Veggie Power Smoothie
1pm	**Juice 2:** Ruby Tuesday
4pm	**Juice 3:** Ruby Tuesday
7pm	**Juice 4:** Veggie Power Smoothie
Any time	**Herbal Teas** (fresh or tea bags)
Any time	**Hunger SOS** (optional, in case your stomach is rumbling)

DAY 3

9:55am	**Ginger Shot** (The Healthy Espresso)
10am	**Juice 1:** Berry Banana Crunch
1pm	**Juice 2:** The Green Refresher
4pm	**Juice 3:** The Green Refresher
7pm	**Juice 4:** Berry Banana Crunch
Any time	**Herbal Teas** (fresh or tea bags)
Any time	**Hunger SOS!** (optional and better than eating your hand off)

DAY 4

9:55am	**Ginger Shot** (The Healthy Espresso)
10am	**Juice 1:** Nature's Super Blend
1pm	**Juice 2:** Minty Sunshine
4pm	**Juice 3:** Minty Sunshine
7pm	**Juice 4:** Nature's Super Blend
Any time	**Herbal Teas** (fresh or tea bags)
Any time	**Hunger SOS!** (optional anytime the need arises)

DAY 5

9:55am	**Ginger Shot** (The Healthy Espresso)
10am	**Juice 1:** Sweet Beet Smoothie
1pm	**Juice 2:** Pear 'n' Parsnip
4pm	**Juice 3:** Pear 'n' Parsnip
7pm	**Juice 4:** Sweet Beet Smoothie
Any time	**Herbal Teas** (fresh or tea bags)
Any time	**Hunger SOS** (optional, if you feel you're about to eat a horse!)

THE
SHOPPING
LIST

ALL THE JUICY STUFF YOU'LL NEED FOR YOUR FIVE-DAY JUICE PROGRAMME AND BEYOND

12

ESSENTIAL JUICY TOOLKIT

Clearly you are going to need a juicer and a blender to do this programme. I have already mentioned on page 113 how important it is to get the right one for you but for more information go to Chapter 20, So Which Juicer Is Best, Jase?, on page 255. Also check the Juice Master website, **www.juicemaster.com**, as things are always changing in the juicing market and the right juicer will make the difference between juicing for a week and making juicing part of your daily life.

Blenders, unlike juicers, are often the same, and all do pretty much the same job. Many people with a Philips juicer often buy a Philips blender as they match in their kitchen! But the best blender I've found on the market is the Vitamix. The makers will often refer to it as a juicer, but it's not, it's a blender – a really, really good blender, but it's not a juicer.

A juicer extracts the juice from the fibres, whereas a blender simply blends the fibres and the juice together. Most people already own a blender of some kind, but many still don't own a juicer (however, it is worth looking in your cupboard as you may have purchased one at the Good Food Show after a few too many wine tastings and forgotten that you bought it!). Seriously though, do not compromise on your juicer if you don't have to, as a good juicer makes ALL the difference.

When you look at the price of some juicers and start adding up the price of the juicer, the blender and the fruits and vegetables, it may seem like an expensive five days! But think about it differently … if you are doing one of Jamie Oliver's 30-minute meals, you don't add up the price of the pots and pans needed to make it happen, do you? Juicing is different because it's still new to many people, so a juicer is still considered an added purchase. However just like pots and pans, once bought, you'll use your juicer again and again and it will hopefully become a lifestyle change catalyst. The vast majority of people who do my plans are so blown away by the results that juicing either becomes an everyday event or they do this plan (or one similar) a few times a year. So, although it can appear to be an expensive initial investment, next time you do the plan you will only need to buy the beautiful fruits and vegetables.

Talking of which, you will of course need the right produce. The following can all be purchased from most local markets or supermarkets, but you will need to order the Power Greens (previously Ultimate Super Food) and Hunger SOS natural energy bars online, so please allow time for delivery.

We have just linked up with a great company who have made ordering the ingredients for the 5lbs in 5 Days Juice Detox Diet a whole lot easier. Now there's no more adding individual items to your shopping cart; just one click and everything you need gets sent to you. It even includes five raw energy Hunger SOS bars. You even have the option to add the Power Greens from their website, making the whole process that much easier. Visit www.juicemasterfreshbox.com.

Alternatively, if you want to shop at another store or buy everything organic, or you're not in the UK, here's the list of everything you need for the full five days:

The Shopping List

apples (preferably Golden Delicious) x 25
avocados (medium, ripe) x 3 (also see Hunger SOS)
banana x 1 (also see Hunger SOS)
basil x 1 small pot (8 x stems)
beetroot, raw (small/medium bulbs) x 4
blackberries x 1 small punnet
broccoli x 1 head
carrots (medium, preferably organic) x 18
celery x 1 head
courgettes (zucchini) (medium) x 2
cucumbers x 3
fennel (small bulb) x 1
ginger, root (large claw) 14 cm
green bell pepper x 1
kale x 1 small bag
lemon (wax-free if possible) x 1
limes (wax-free if possible) x 7
mint x 1 large pot (16 x stems)
mixed berries, e.g. blueberries, raspberries, strawberries, blackberries –
    if fresh x 1 small punnet or if frozen x 1 small bag
mixed seeds, e.g. sunflower, pumpkin, sesame and linseed x 1 small bag
natural teas
natural yoghurt (bio-live if possible) x 150g
oranges x 4
parsnips (medium) x 2
pears (preferably Conference) x 6
pineapples (medium) x 2
spinach x 3 large bags
sugar snap peas or **beans** x 1 packet

BE FLEXIBLE!

You will notice that many of the recipes contain ginger and lime. This is because ginger has such a vast array of incredible health properties that you almost cannot have enough, and lime helps to slow down the oxidation of the juice. However, if you don't like ginger or lime for whatever reason, you can simply leave them out. The same goes for any of the smaller, more obscure, ingredients, such as fennel. If you can though, do the programme as it is.

Personally, I hate broccoli and celery, but in a juice, when mixed with other juices, such as apple, they taste good – so please try the juices first before you adjust them!

BE PREPARED!

For five days, the only thing you will be drinking, other than the juices and smoothies, will be water and natural teas. So you may wish to buy some bottled mineral water (still or naturally sparkling) and treat yourself to some beautiful teas, such as Pukka or Tea Pigs, or of course the classic Twinings brand. I tend to go for any mint variety and chamomile, but the choice is yours. Another great option is to buy some extra fresh mint and add a couple of stems to a cup of nearly boiling water. Freshly sliced lemon and ginger with near boiling water is also fantastic. You can also add a spoonful of honey (preferably active Manuka) to your tea.

The following shopping list is optional and flexible:

The Flexi Shopping List

ginger, root (small claw) x 1

herbal tea x 1 or 2 boxes

honey (preferably Manuka) x 1 pot

Juice Master's Power Greens* x 1 bottle (previously Ultimate Super Food), available from www.juicemaster.com. They are of premium quality and do not contain any cheap fillers, although feel free to buy a different brand such as Udos, which are very good.

lemon x 3

mineral water – still or sparkling x 5 bottles

mint x 1 pot

Each day you are also allowed ONE of the following if you need a Hunger SOS, so adjust your shopping list accordingly:

avocado

banana

Juice Master's Juice in a Bar*

Juice Master Simply Nude Bar*

Juice Master's Juice in a Bar energy bar won the *Best New Food Product of the Year* award and for good reason. Juice Master energy bars are made from the finest 100 per cent natural raw ingredients, with no added sugars, chemicals, preservatives, additives or anything nasty. I developed these bars because it was so incredibly hard to find a 100 per cent healthy and very genuine snack.

If you're in the UK, get everything with one click at www.juicemasterfreshbox.com.

The
JUICY
RECIPES

ALL THE JUICES

13

EVERY DAY

GINGER SHOT: THE HEALTHY ESPRESSO

There are certain things you have to experience rather than read about, and the Ginger Shot is one of those things. This is a little shot with a very big impact. I call it 'The Healthy Espresso' and it will certainly give you a very sharp wake-up call first thing in the morning. I recommend downing this baby in one (like people do with a shot of tequila) before your first smoothie and enjoying the rush as your senses are assaulted by a completely natural high. This little baby comes courtesy of Kasper, founder of Joe & The Juice, a wonderful juice bar chain from Denmark, now in the UK too.

Juicy Ingredients
½ large apple (Golden Delicious ideally, but any will do)
2–3 cm chunk root ginger (be generous!)

Make it in a Shot!

Simply juice the apple and ginger, cutting the apple in half and sandwiching the ginger between the two apple pieces (this guarantees a maximum amount of juice from the ginger). Down this in one and say good morning to your senses!

The Little Shot With a Massive Impact!

Regardless of whether I am on a particular juice plan or not, I make sure that the first nutrition to hit my system everyday is a Ginger Shot. This super shot was responsible for curing my severe hay fever (it's a wonderful natural anti-histamine), but it's also a natural antibiotic, a wonderful decongestant, a natural anti-inflammatory, and great for travel sickness; it also inhibits the formation of blood clots and helps to lower cholesterol. Ginger is loaded with minerals, including copper, potassium, sodium, iron, calcium, zinc, phosphorus and magnesium. Ginger juice is simply one of the finest health tonics on earth and a ginger shot each morning will go a long way in helping to prevent many health issues. The ginger shot also contains freshly extracted apple juice, which is rich in potassium, phosphorous and magnesium. Potassium works beautifully with magnesium to help regulate heart functions.

DAY 1

TURBO ... WITH A KICK!

This recipe is a twist on the now infamous Turbo Charge Smoothie. It's odd to think that a smoothie can be famous, but due to the success of my *Turbo-charge Your Life In 14 Days* book, and to making this recipe with Katie Price (aka Jordan) for a fitness and health DVD, it is. The Turbo smoothie was the first smoothie recipe bringing together freshly extracted juice with a blended avocado to appear in a book. It's now the bedrock for all my juice plans as it turns a nutritious drink into a meal. The combination just works, and if you have never drunk an avocado before you are about to be enlightened ... and hopefully converted!

Juicy Ingredients

2 Golden Delicious apples

¼ medium pineapple (depending on your juicer, with or without the skin)

1 handful spinach

½ lime (wax-free and peeled)

½ stick celery

3 cm chunk cucumber

1 cm chunk root ginger

¼ medium avocado

1 small handful ice cubes

How to Create This Creamy Juice Master Piece

Juice all the ingredients except the avocado and ice. Pour the juice into a blender along with the avocado flesh and ice and blend until smooth.

What's the Kick?

As a change from the traditional Turbo recipe, I have added a nice chunk of ginger. As the name suggests this gives it a real kick. This smoothie is rich in chlorophyll which helps to oxygenate the blood while alkalizing the body. Turbo also contains all of the essential amino acids (the building blocks for protein); it's loaded with essential fatty acids, such as Omega-3 3, and extremely rich in the vast majority of vitamins and minerals required for optimum health, including vitamin E, which is amazing for the skin and rarely found in fruits.

Well, I Never Knew That About Avocados!

★ Avocados have the highest protein content of any fruit. Avocados contain more potassium than bananas.

★ One avocado contains 81 mcg of lutein, an important nutrient for healthy eyes.

★ Once an avocado is picked, it takes between seven and ten days to ripen. Keeping it in the refrigerator will slow down the ripening process, while putting it in a paper bag with a ripe apple or banana will speed up the process.

★ On average, 60 million pounds of guacamole are eaten every Super Bowl Sunday, enough to cover a football field more than 20 feet thick.

DAY 1

THE NATURAL ENERGIZER

Creamy, sweet and mellow pineapple juice is the perfect complement to the mineral-rich juice from the cucumber, spinach, sugar snap peas and courgette. This juice is then taken to the next level by adding a hint of fennel and a dash of zesty lime. Not only is this juice creamy and delicious, but unlike artificial energy drinks (which ultimately rob your body of nutrients, cause stress to your vital organs and send you on a rollercoaster of refined sugar energy highs and lows) this juice will provide energy in a very natural way. *Say 'high' to nature!*

Juicy Stuff Needed for This Natural Energy Boost

¼ medium pineapple (with or without the skin, depending on your juicer)

I large handful spinach

¼ medium cucumber

½ medium courgette/zucchini

I cm slice/chunk fennel

I5 sugar snap peas or beans

½ lime (with the skin on)

I small handful ice cubes

Couldn't Be Easier

Simply juice all the ingredients and pour over ice.

Why Drink This Baby?

When you speak to people about their health, one of the main things most people crave more of is energy. Unfortunately most people use refined sugars and junk food as a way of providing their energy boost and therefore run on nervous energy rather than genuine energy. This beautiful juice provides a natural lift while providing the body with key nutrients, such as vitamins C, B and K, as well as iron, calcium and potassium.

Well, I Never Knew That About Sugar Snap Peas!

★ A 100-calorie serving of sugar snap peas contains more protein than a whole egg or tablespoon of peanut butter.

★ Sugar snap peas are from the legume family. Legumes are plants that produce pods containing edible, fleshy seeds.

★ 1 cup of sugar snap peas equals just 45 calories.

★ Sugar snap peas are a good source of vitamins A, C, thiamin, riboflavin and niacin.

★ Fresh pods have 150 per cent more vitamin C than garden peas.

★ Sugar snap peas are also good in many other essential B-complex vitamins such as pantothenic acid, niacin, thiamin and pyridoxine. They are rich source of many minerals such as calcium, iron, copper, zinc, selenium, phosphorus, potassium and manganese.

DAY 2

VEGGIE POWER SMOOTHIE

Deep, green, chlorophyll-rich spinach, kale and broccoli, mixed with the cool tones of cucumber, celery, apple and lemon juice, all blended together with soft, creamy avocado. This super-green smoothie is surprisingly light, refreshing and yet at the same time beautifully filling. Just what you need on Day 2!

What Do We Need to Get Powered Up?

2 apples (Golden Delicious ideally but any will do)
1 large handful spinach
1 large handful kale
½ lemon (wax-free with the skin on)
½ stick celery
¼ medium cucumber
2cm chunk broccoli stem
½ medium avocado
1 small handful ice cubes

How to Produce the Power

Juice all the ingredients except the avocado and ice. Pour the juice into a blender along with the avocado flesh and ice and blend until smooth.

Why Is This So Powerful?

This is a superb smoothie to start and finish your day with as it contains nature's numero uno super food – avocado. This rich and creamy fruit contains essential fats, which not only keep you satiated, but also help to prevent cardiovascular disease. When it comes to veggie power, green is where it's at, combining kale, spinach, and broccoli to make this powerhouse of pure green nutrition. This combination is extremely rich in chlorophyll and essential amino acids, vitamins, minerals and natural sugars. As the late eminent juicing pioneer Dr Norman Walker said, 'in raw spinach juice, nature has furnished man with the finest organic material for cleansing, reconstruction and regeneration of the intestinal tract' – and that's just the spinach.

Well, I Never Knew That About Kale!

★ Kale has good anti-inflammatory properties which come from Omega-3 and vitamin K. Kale helps to regulate the body's inflammatory process. Regular intake of kale can reduce health problems related to inflammation and chronic inflammation.

★ Kale belongs to the same family as cabbage, Brussels sprouts and collards.

★ Vitamin K plays important roles in preventing neuronal damage in the brain and improving bone health. Zeaxanthin is known for eye-health promoting benefits.

★ Kale is a useful vegetable for good skin. Antioxidant nutrients in kale promote skin health. Kale is often used to reduce skin blemishes including acne.

DAY 2

RUBY TUESDAY

My tribute to the truly incredible Rolling Stones – I was lucky enough to see them at a small gig at the Brixton Academy and mind-blowing is the only word I can use. In case you don't know, 'Ruby Tuesday' was released in January 1967.

Now, on with the juice! Rich, nutritious beetroot and carrot juice combined with sweet creamy pineapple juice, a mellow fresh hit of basil and a little cheeky kick of ginger. It may come as no surprise that this juice comes on day 2, which for most starting on a Monday, will indeed be a Ruby Tuesday. This is one of the nicest juices on the programme – hope you agree.

Juicy Ingredients

¼ medium pineapple (with or without the skin, depending on your juicer)
2 medium carrots
I small bulb raw beetroot
I–2 cm chunk root ginger 4 sprigs fresh basil
I small handful ice cubes
no brown sugar (sorry, just a little ref to a Stones track)

How to Create

Juice all the ingredients but make sure you sandwich the basil and ginger in between other ingredients to ensure maximum juice extraction.

Why Say Hello and Not Goodbye to This Ruby Tuesday?

Beetroot is currently one of the most talked-about vegetables in terms of its nutritional benefits and there have been several studies conducted globally about the effects of drinking beetroot juice. The conclusion of all these studies is that the high level of nitrates found in beetroot keep the blood vessels dilated, meaning that high blood pressure is reduced and stamina in both the elderly and also athletes is improved due to the increased oxygen uptake capability. This juice is also loaded with vitamins B and C and beta-carotene, as well as calcium, magnesium, iron, sodium, potassium and magnesium.

Well, I Never Knew That About Basil!

★ Basil leaves contain essential oils such as eugenol, citronellol, linalool, citral, limonene and terpineol. These are known to have anti-inflammatory and anti-bacterial properties.

★ Basil contains exceptionally high levels of beta-carotene, cryptoxanthin, lutein and zeaxanthin. These compounds help act as protective scavengers against oxygen-derived free radicals and reactive oxygen species (ROS) that play a role in ageing and various disease processes.

★ 100g of fresh herb leaves contain astoundingly 5275mg or 175 per cent of the daily required doses of vitamin A.

★ Vitamin K in basil is essential for many coagulant factors in the blood and plays a vital role in the bone-strengthening function by helping mineralization process in the bones.

DAY 3

BERRY BANANA CRUNCH

Sweet scrumptious mixed berries blended with freshly extracted apple juice, natural yoghurt* and creamy banana, then naturally fortified with a generous sprinkling of mixed seeds, all loaded with essential fatty acids. It's creamy, fruity, extremely nutritious, crunchy and so, so filling – exactly what you need on Day 3.

* If vegan please either use more banana or swap for soya yoghurt.

What to Mix

2 apples (Golden Delicious ideally or any will do)

2 handfuls mixed berries e.g. blueberries, blackberries, raspberries, strawberries (fresh or frozen**)

2 tbsps natural yoghurt (use soya if vegan, or leave out altogether if you prefer and use a whole banana instead)

½ Fairtrade banana

1 tbsp mixed seeds (these usually come in a mixed bag containing sunflower, pumpkin, sesame and linseed, but any variation on this will be fine)

1 handful ice cubes

**Feel free to buy a bag of frozen mixed berries even if they contain slightly different berries. Alternatively, if a certain berry is in season and you want to use just one type, again feel free. Personally I love this recipe with just two handfuls of fresh blackberries when they are in season.

How to Make

Juice the apples and pour into the blender. Add all the berries, natural yoghurt, banana, seeds and ice and blend for just a few seconds. Top Tip: if you use frozen berries there is no need to add extra ice to the blender.

NB: If you don't like bits in your juice or a little crunch, leave out the seeds.

Why Mix It Up?

Mixed seeds are an incredible source of iron, polyunsaturated fats, thiamine, phosphorous, selenium, copper, magnesium, folate, niacin, vitamin E … the list goes on. They are an excellent supplement to your diet as they are a nutrition powerhouse and, unlike most fruits and vegetables, they also contain Omega-3 and 6 EFAs (Essential Fatty Acids). On top of this, the recipe contains banana, which is one of our best sources of potassium, an essential mineral for maintaining normal blood pressure and heart function. And then there are the berries, the richest antioxidant fruits on earth.

Going Bananas!

★ In terms of nutrition, it's hard to beat the humble banana – it's the most perfect on-the-go food in the world.

★ They contain no fat, are low in calories and very high in B6, fibre and potassium. They also contain nice amounts of phosphorus, magnesium, calcium, iron, zinc, copper, selenium, vitamins A, B1, B2, C, E and K and niacin.

★ The banana plant is a herb, which makes the banana itself a berry!

DAY 3

THE GREEN REFRESHER

Fresh apple and succulent thick pear juice, combined with cool, cleansing cucumber juice, mineral-abundant spinach juice, super healthy broccoli juice and a little cheeky twist of lime. Nutritious yet extremely delicious!

What's In It?

1 apple

1 pear (Conference pears are best. You want hard pears as you get more juice.)

¼ medium cucumber

2 large handfuls spinach

2cm chunk broccoli stem

1 lime (peeled, but keep the white pith on. If you don't want to be 'slapped' with lime, feel free to add just half a lime.)

1 small handful ice cubes

How to Get Refreshed

Juice everything at once but try and sandwich the lime, broccoli and spinach in between the apple, pear and cucumber to ensure maximum juice extraction. (If using the Fusion juicer, please juice everything one at a time as the low induction motor will stop if you pack things in.) Pour over ice and enjoy.

Why Broccoli Juice?

Broccoli is renowned as a true 'super food' and one of the reasons for this is due to its incredible vitamin content. The broccoli alone found in this juice will supply you with over 100 per cent of your RDA of vitamins C and K as well as over 25 per cent of your RDA of vitamin A. Broccoli is also able to aid your body's detoxification system, as it contains glucoraphanin, gluconasturtiin and glucobrassicin. This dynamic trio is able to support all steps in the body's detox process, including activation, neutralization and elimination of unwanted contaminants. Broccoli is without doubt well deserving of its title as a true super food. Personally I am not a fan of eating raw broccoli (I don't know many who are), which is why juicing is such a wonderful way to get the goodness while not having to eat it!

Well, I Never Knew That About the Humble Pear!

★ Pears are one of the very low-calorie fruits, providing 58 calories per 100g. Pears are a moderate source of antioxidant flavonoid phytonutrients such as beta-carotene, lutein and zeaxanthin. These compounds, along with vitamin C and A, help protect the body from harmful free radicals.

★ Pears are a good source of minerals such as copper, iron, potassium, manganese and magnesium as well as B-complex vitamins such as folates, riboflavin and pyridoxine (vitamin B6).

★ Various traditional medicines suggest that pears are useful in treating colitis, chronic gall bladder disorders, arthritis and gout.

DAY 4

NATURE'S SUPER BLEND

Delicate, ripe, creamy rich avocado combined with the refreshing juice of mineral-rich vegetables and the delicious soft flavours of fresh velvety apple juice, then infused with a generous kick of zesty lime. There is always at least one juice on a detox that let's you know you're on one. If you want a juice that feels like you have blended nature, this is your baby!

The Ultimate Ingredients

2 apples (Golden Delicious or any of your choice)
I large handful spinach
¼ medium courgette/zucchini
I lime (wax-free and peeled)
2 medium carrots
¼ medium cucumber
2cm chunk broccoli stem
½ stalk celery
¼ green bell pepper
½ medium avocado
I small handful ice cubes

How to Make This Natural Smoothie

Juice all the ingredients except the avocado and ice. Pour the juice into a blender, along with the avocado flesh and ice, and blend until smooth.

Why it's One of Nature's Finest

Contains vitamin A, most of the B vitamins including folic acid, vitamin C, vitamin E, vitamin K, potassium, sodium, zinc, phosphorus, magnesium, calcium, manganese ... the list continues. This smoothie is good for every part of your body from your eyes, your heart and your liver right through to your skin.

Well, I Never Knew That About the Humble Pepper!

★ Peppers are rich in iron, copper, zinc, potassium, manganese, magnesium and selenium. Manganese is used by the body as a co-factor for the antioxidant enzyme superoxide dismutase. Selenium is an antioxidant micro-mineral that acts as a co-factor for enzyme superoxide dismutase.

★ They are also rich in B-complex group of vitamins such as niacin, pyridoxine (vitamin B6), riboflavin and thiamin (vitamin B1). These vitamins are essential in the sense that the body requires them from external sources to replenish. B-complex vitamins facilitate cellular metabolism through various enzymatic functions.

★ And they're rich in vitamin C, containing in some cases twice the amount as an orange.

DAY 4

MINTY SUNSHINE

Take the juiciest oranges you can find and combine them with dense, rich, dark carrots and a large handful of refreshing gorgeous mint. Then finish off with a dash of freshly extracted ginger for a truly divine taste indulgence.

This is such a welcome juice on Day 4; it is one of the tastiest of the week and helps to make sure you complete the five days.

The Lovelies Needed for This Taste Explosion

2 juicy oranges

3 medium dark carrots (the darker the carrot the more nutrients it contains – avoid 'luminous' carrots!)

1–2 cm chunk root ginger4 sprigs fresh mint

1 small handful ice cubes

How to Create the Magic

Peel the oranges, remembering to leave the white pith on, as this is where the majority of the nutrients are to be found. Juice the oranges, carrots, ginger and gorgeous mint. Pour the juice over ice and enjoy.

Why Have This Stupidly Refreshing Juice?

You have never had *real* orange juice until you juice oranges with the pith on through a normal juicer. Most people cut the orange in half and then simply push on a citrus press. When you do this you miss many of the nutrients as a large amount sit within the *pith* just beneath the skin. This not only makes the juice healthier but brings it to another level on the taste front. Carrot juice is famous for it's rich provitamin A content (beta-carotene) but carrot juice is king because it also contains vitamins B,C,E, and K as well many minerals including, calcium, iron, magnesium, potassium and phosphors. The fresh mint and ginger add a great coolness to the taste, but also add plenty on the health front; the ginger alone is antiviral, antibacterial, an anti-histamine and a superb decongestant.

Well, I Never Knew That About Refreshing Mint!

★ Mint was one of the earliest herbs discovered. It has been found in Egyptian tombs dating back to 1,000 BC and has been part of the Chinese pharmacopoeia for even longer.
★ Peppermint is one of the oldest home remedies for indigestion.
★ Today mint is still used to alleviate flatulence and aid digestion.
★ Studies show that peppermint lessens the amount of time food spends in the stomach by stimulating the gastric lining to produce enzymes which aid digestion.

DAY 5

SWEET BEET SMOOTHIE

Deep, dark, yet surprisingly sweet, beetroot juice blended with creamy soft apple juice and delicate amber carrot juice, then infused with decadent, luscious blackberries. This combination is simply divine and you won't believe that a juice with beetroot can taste so sublime. This is without question one of the nicest and most nutritious recipes in the plan. You will feel your arteries breath a sigh of relief as this beauty hits the bloodstream.

Sweet Juicy Ingredients

1 apple (preferably Golden Delicious, but any will do)
2 medium carrots
1 medium bulb raw beetroot
1 large handful blackberries (or you can use other dark berries, fresh or frozen)
1 small handful ice cubes

How to Sweeten Up Your Beets

Juice the apple, carrots and beetroot and pour the juice into a blender along with the berries and ice. Blend for a few seconds and pour into a beautiful glass.

Why Sweet Beet?

Blackberries are an 'aggregate fruit' composed of many individual drupelets. These drupelets contribute extra skin, seeds and pectin, making them among the highest fibre content plants known. Blackberries are also naturally antibacterial and the handful in this recipe provides you with 50 per cent of your RDA of vitamin C, 36 per cent of your RDA of vitamin K and 47 per cent of your RDA of manganese. Raw beetroot is an excellent source of niacin, nitrate, folate, potassium, iron, magnesium and manganese. The antioxidants present in beetroot can help protect against coronary heart disease and strokes as well as lowering high blood pressure.

Well, I Never Knew That About Sweet Blackberries

★ Blackberries contain many health-promoting flavonoid polyphenolic antioxidants such as lutein, zeaxanthin and beta-carotene. Blackberries have an ORAC value (oxygen radical absorbance capacity, a measure of antioxidant strength) of about 5347μmol TE per 100g.

★ Blackberries contain a good amount of minerals like potassium, manganese, copper and magnesium. Copper is required in the bone metabolism as well as in production of white and red blood cells.

★ Blackberries also contain moderate levels of the B-complex group of vitamins and very good amounts of pyridoxine, niacin, pantothenic acid, riboflavin and folic acid. These vitamins are acting as cofactors to help the body metabolize carbohydrates, proteins and fats.

DAY 5

PEAR 'N' PARSNIP

If you think this recipe won't 'float your boat' or that it sounds a little weird, then please have faith and prepare to be surprised. This is a really special and unique juice that will give you a new-found respect for the so-often-overlooked parsnip. If you think they are just good for roasting or mashing then think again as parsnips are an excellent addition to any juice.

Juicy Ingredients

I apple (preferably Golden Delicious, but any will do)
2 pears (conference pears make a lovely juice, but any will do – just make sure they are hard as you get more juice)
I medium parsnip
½ lime (peeled, but keep the white pith on)
4 sprigs fresh mint
I small handful Ice Cubes

How to Make This Medley?

Juice the ingredients by placing the lime and mint in between the pears and parsnip to ensure maximum juice extraction. Pour over ice and enjoy.

Why Pair this Unlikely Pear?

Pear juice is loaded with pectin, a soluble fibre that has been found to act like a gel in the intestine, trapping toxins and waste and sweeping them out of the system. Soluble fibre has been found to lower cholesterol levels and regulate blood sugar levels. Parsnips are packed with vitamin C, folate, calcium, magnesium, potassium and manganese. One medium parsnip contains 29 per cent of your RDA of vitamin C and 8 per cent of your RDA of potassium. Mint is a magic little herb renowned for relaxing your digestive tract, easing symptoms from digestive disorders such as bloating, abdominal pain and IBS. It's also wonderful for freshening your breath!

Well, I Never Knew That About the Little Parsnip

★ Parsnips contain many poly-acetylene antioxidants such as falcarinol, falcarindiol, panaxydiol and methyl-falcarindiol.

★ Several research studies from scientists at Newcastle University found that compounds contained in parsnips have anti-inflammatory, anti-fungal and anti-cancer function and offer protection from colon cancer and acute lymphoblastic leukaemia (ALL).

★ Parsnips are rich in many B-complex groups of vitamins such as folic acid, vitamin B6 (pyridoxine), thiamin and pantothenic acid as well as vitamin K and vitamin E.

★ Parsnips have good levels of minerals including iron, calcium, copper, potassium, manganese and phosphorus. Potassium is an important component of cell and body fluids that helps control heart rate and blood pressure by countering the effects of sodium.

Your
JUICY
JOURNAL

14

Some people find it extremely useful to keep a journal of their progress and to make notes throughout the week. You may find it easier to keep your diary via your smart digital device these days, but if you want to go old school and write on paper, here are five pages to keep notes of your progress.

Before you start, it is important to know your weight and measurements. This is so you can see the incredible changes that will happen in just five days. I advise you to weigh yourself on the morning of Day 1 (usually a Monday) *before* you have a juice and again on the morning of Day 6 (usually a Saturday), again *before* you consume anything.

Your starting juicy statistics

Weight

Chest

Waist

Body Fat %

Hips

DAY 1

The first day can often be one of the easiest for people as it's when they are really fired up. For others though, day 1 can be the hardest. Some people may get headaches and feel tired; this is perfectly normal and will go in a couple of days. The key to day 1 is make sure you have all your juices on time and to make sure you use your HUNGER SOS if needed.

Use this space to jot down any feelings you may have. You may find it is cathartic and helps the process immensely.

DAY 2

I refer to this as Tetchy Tuesday, as this is the day where most have 'their day'. Everyone will have at least one day where they feel not right and for the vast majority it's Tetchy Tuesday. Re-read the MIND OVER FATTER chapter in times of need. Jot down how you are feeling and ask yourself, where does it hurt if at all? What is so hard about it? If it's just a headache and a 'false hunger' or two, put it into perspective and remind yourself why you are doing this.

DAY 3

Final day of any withdrawal from refined sugars, caffeine and the such. I describe this as 'the junk food terrorist' and he's about for a few days, as long as you don't feed him he's gone after close of play today. Write down what's happening and make sure you have all of your juices, on time!

DAY 4

Two more days and it is these two days where you really start to feel the difference. If you have struggled at all over the past three days, now is the time to start reaping the rewards. Once again, jot down how you feel.

DAY 5

This is it – THE FINAL DAY! Please do not weigh yourself until tomorrow morning to see the full impact of your Juice Detox Diet. This is also the day to prepare for the next stage of your new healthier lifestyle. Start your day with a fresh juice tomorrow, and then move onto a nice light lunch and a Low H.I dinner. By now you should be craving low H.I foods, not refined fat, salt and sugar. It is Friday night for most and it's the final night, so don't think 4.5 days is enough – this is a 5-day juice detox, not 4.5! If you are going to do it, do it 100 per cent. If you want to remind yourself of what to do next, then re-read LOW-H.I WAY OF LIFE.

CONGRATULATIONS!

Your closing juicy statistics

Weight

Chest

Waist

Body Fat %

Hips

Part 4

THE ROUGH
AFTER PLAN

Here I would like to share a few key principles to help you to not only keep the weight off, but to carry on in the right way in order to have a healthy body and be a healthy weight for life. If you already have the 5lbs in 5 Days app, or the book *Turbo-charge Your Life In 14 Days*, you will already have an idea of what to do after a juice exclusive programme, but what follows are the fundamental points everyone should know.

The very essence of what I teach is *Freedom from the Diet Trap* and freedom is exactly what is vital for a healthy mind and body. You need to be free to eat and drink what you want, not what you have been programmed to eat and drink by what I describe as BIG FOOD and BIG DRINK companies. You need to be completely free to eat and drink what you feel like when you feel like it. The key, of course, is to change your mindset so that the so-called foods and drinks which may have made up the vast majority of your diet before the 5lbs in 5 Days programme are no longer as appealing as they once were. The aim is for you to want the good stuff the vast majority of the time, so that you're not operating with a *diet mentality* but rather with a *freedom mentality*. This all means that nothing is off the table – nothing! It means we need to start to understand that the body can deal with a certain amount of anything and that it's the ratio of that anything that counts.

When people talk about a *balanced diet* and *everything in moderation*, what they usually mean is, *'let's eat crap most of the time but every now and then let's have an apple!'* We need to not only change the ratio of junk to good, but also the speed we eat at and the amount of food we consume. The fact is, we simply do not require anywhere near the amount of food we have been programmed to believe we need. Please remember, it is in the financial interest of BIG FOOD and BIG DRINK to sell you more and more food. This is why they lace virtually everything they sell with the Holy Grails of the *trigger you to eat more* substances – FAT, SALT and SUGAR. These cause *additional hungers* and leave us feeling empty when we remove them from our life, thus creating a desire for more of the same, rather than an apple. This is also why some people struggle on the first three days on the programme, and why it can prove challenging, as they are withdrawing from *drug-like* foods and drinks. This is why the ratio is key, and having spent a full five days without the big three (refined fat, refined salt, refined sugar) and having flooded your body with vital nutrients, the last thing I am hoping you want to do is cram loads of the big three back into your body. You can do what you like, but after five days on fresh veggie and fruit juice, I am hoping you have moved from a diet mentality of 'I want but I can't have' to a freedom mentality of 'I can but I don't want.'

DESIGN YOUR OWN DIET

I haven't provided a specific plan as the vast majority of people will do their own thing and freestyle it from here on in. When I talk about designing your own diet, I don't mean diet in its restrictive sense, but as the word was originally designed. If you were to describe the diet of any wild animal, you wouldn't be talking about them being on a diet but rather the food they choose to eat all the time. Unlike wild animals, where all of a particular species eat exactly the same food (Eucalyptus leaves for Koala bears, bamboo for pandas, etc.) our diets vary greatly from one person to another. This is why it is important to design your own diet and set a programme that works for you.

THE 5-2-5 PLAN

Some people will continue to have a nice thick veggie-based smoothie for breakfast, one for lunch and a simple evening meal (which works beautifully, if you are looking to get to your ideal weight) and some will choose to eat anything for two days a week and juice for five until they reach their ideal weight. This is known as the 5-2-5 plan and it's highly effective!

This is not the same as the popular 5:2 diet where you eat anything for five days a week and then consume 600 calories for two days a week. This is where you have five full days of juice and two days of anything. Many people I know who had a lot of weight to lose have used this option and found it very effective.

Others will juice in the morning, have a nice light lunch and then a protein-rich dinner, which is a good overall diet for life. It's different for everyone who chooses to freestyle it. For those who don't want to design their diet and really want a set plan with recipes to follow after the juicing, I would advise reading something like *Turbo-charge Your Life in 14 Days*. This has proved a wonderful follow-on programme and is great for those who just need some ideas before they then go on to design their own diet. It can also have some amazing knock-on results, as this recent Facebook post illustrates:

Jason! Since starting my new year with your 7lbs in 7 days program: I felt so darn fabulous that I went on to complete a full MONTH of juicing. And currently am still juicing every single day and loving it – inspiring those around me – very much thanks to you! ... Your Turbo Salad makes my world go round! I crave it literally every single day ... 3 0 lbs down now, 4 jean sizes gone for good (I burned my Fat-jeans so I can't fall back on them! lol) Down 23 inches! How can I thank you for changing my life?

Laura

And here's another example for good measure:

Day 11 today of my new life, and after 10 days of almost 100 per cent juicing (and very low HI foods when I did eat) I am a stone lighter than when I started. And it is soooo easy. Thanks Jason for all the inspiration and passion, I know that this is something I can keep doing for the rest of my healthy life!

Johanna

If you are like most people, by the time you reach Day 5 the things you thought you would have craved at the end are not the things you are actually craving at all. The vast majority of people are very surprised as they are yearning for things like lean proteins, salads, vegetables, soups and just all-round good natural food. However, whatever diet you design for your life, even if that includes some of the big three (as it will from time to time, no doubt; we are all human after all!) here are two key concepts I would highly recommend living by. Adopt these babies and you'll be good to go for life ...

THE Low-H.I. WAY OF LIFE

15

I have been researching diet and nutrition for over 15 years now and, as most people find with this subject, the more I study the more complicated it gets and ultimately the more confusing it becomes.

Food labels have become so confusing over the years that you almost need a degree in science just to decipher what they mean. Even the government's 'traffic light' system is flawed on almost every level. I think the biggest problem stems from Professor Ancel Keys and his Seven Countries Study. It is solely because of this one study that, even to this day, people believe that the main cause of heart disease and getting fat is saturated fat. This is why for many years people have been studying food labels to discover their fat content. and why to this day we have TV doctors telling everyone on breakfast and primetime TV to cut down on fat to save their lives and avoid being overweight. It is only in recent years that *refined white sugar* has finally been recognized as the true culprit in causing both heart disease and obesity. Having said that, if you were to do a straw poll down your local high street, you would find that the vast majority of people still believe that FAT makes you FAT and gives you heart disease.

It is interesting to observe that Ancel Keys studied 22 countries, yet his study became known as the Seven Countries

Study. This is because, as often happens, Ancel cherry-picked the data to meet his hypothesis in order to shift it from a hunch to a fact. The results from Japan, Italy, Great Britain, Australia, Canada and the US were left in, and the rest thrown to one side. When researchers analysed his data using all 22 countries, the link between fat and heart disease totally vanished. Despite this, the anti-fat propaganda went full steam ahead and the pushing of refined grains and sugars took over. It is also interesting to know that for over ten years sugar was completely left off the agenda at the WHO (World Health Organization). Too many people with vested interests in the sugar industry at the time were to blame.

The challenge we all face is that *new* studies are coming out all the time and it's almost impossible to a) keep up and b) know what to believe. One minute butter is the devil and margarine is the best thing since (and on) sliced bread. Then we hear margarine is about a molecule away from plastic and revert back to butter. One study says eggs are great and another says more than three a week will give you a heart attack. We were told animal protein was off the table, now it's back on. My conclusion is to strip it all down and simplify everything.

THERE'S ALWAYS ANOTHER WAY!

I live by one main mantra: there's always another way. Not only do I believe there is always another way, but I also believe there's always an easier way too. In my opinion, nothing has become more over-complicated than the area of diet and nutrition. I believe this has happened so that people can have letters after their name and feel important. It takes six years to become a qualified dietician – YES, SIX YEARS! That's six years to study what we should be eating to live a long, healthy, slim and disease-free life. Is it just me or is that slightly nuts? Every single wild animal knows exactly what to eat, without one single day of studying and without a single surf on the internet, just to check. This is called 'instinct' and is something we all have.

Our natural instinct has clearly been taken over by BIG FOOD and BIG DRINK who effectively design our diet for us in the name of profit, but I would argue we still very much have that instinct. It is hard to recognize it when we are constantly putting addictive foods into our bloodstream causing us to crave the big three (fat, salt and sugar), but it's very much there. In fact I would argue that even the most prolific junk food addict instinctively knows exactly what to eat and drink to live a long, healthy, slim and disease-free life. They may not do it, due to their overriding addiction, but clearly they know what to do. The good news is that after five days of pure *live* juices you start to move instinctively towards what the body truly needs and, because the overriding addiction is gone, you are free to design your diet and eat freely.

THE NO-LABEL DIET

One of the most commonly asked questions I have had over the years is 'what am I looking for on the label?' It took me many years to have that light-bulb moment and realize it's not what's on the label; it's the fact that it has a label!

Instinctively we should all be eating a No-Label Diet. I am referring to a diet of food which if found in nature wouldn't require a label; such as fruits, vegetables, nuts, seeds, fish, lean proteins and so on. If your diet consisted of at least 80 per cent 'no label foods' and if 50 per cent of that was high water content foods, such as fruits, vegetables (and their juices), soups, salads and vegetables, 30 per cent proteins such as fish, nuts and seeds, 10 per cent whole grains and 10 per cent 'party food' – you'd fly.

Clearly when I talk about 'no label foods' I am not talking about all food that doesn't have a label. I still don't understand why there are such stringent laws when it comes to packaging foods and how they are labelled, and yet you can seemingly serve anything from a van at 2am with no label. Burgers in your supermarket have been labelled so that you know what they contain, yet if you get a hot dog in the cinema or a burger from a van at the footie game, there's no label required. So when I talk about 'no label' I am not talking about that kind of no-label food. In fact this type of food should have its own category – mystery food – as what's in it is often a complete mystery (as we all found out in the UK in 2013 when beef burgers were found to be horse burgers!). Take a rubbery Chicken Kiev for example – it's often not exactly chicken and it certainly never came from Russia. A hot dog, what's in it? If it's a mystery, DON'T EAT IT!

THE LOW-H.I. WAY OF LIFE

An even easier description of what we should all be eating is Low H.I. (Low Human Intervention). It's a lifestyle I do my best to adhere to a great deal of the time. Low H.I. simply means foods and drinks that have had low human intervention before getting to you. In other words, it is food as close to nature intended as possible. This doesn't mean you have to eat Low H.I. all the time, but it's a nice instant overview of what you should be eating.

Now there are certain categories within the H.I. range, such as No H.I., Low Low H.I., Low H.I. and High H.I., but until I finish the main Low-H.I. Diet book, these will have to wait. For now here's a very quick overview and explanation.

Low-H.I. living is not about becoming a vegan or vegetarian (each to their own on that one), it's about making sure that whatever you eat, it hasn't been interfered with too much by humans. If you do eat meat, then ask yourself, 'Is it Low H.I.?' In other words, is the chicken free range/organic, or is it one dose of chemicals away from a science experiment! If you eat fish, is it Low H.I.? Does it look like a piece of fish or is it a bunch of fish parts from many different fish in breadcrumbs? If you are eating tomatoes, are they organic or at least looking like a nice dark ripe tomato, or just a load of squashed chemical-rich tomatoes that have been mixed with sugar and other junk to form a ketchup? If you want bread, is it Low H.I.? Is it as close to the grain as possible or has it been refined, bleached and loaded with sugar, yeast and salt until it looks more like a sponge?

I could give a million examples but the beauty of Low H.I. living is that it is pretty much self-explanatory. Whatever no-label food you eat, you simply ask yourself, 'is it Low H.I.?' There will be some people out there who want to eat a No-H.I. diet.

No-H.I. living is where you pick an apple from the tree yourself in an organic field. This is just a little too much to ask for the average person and as far as I'm concerned, life's too short. You don't, after all, want to spend your one and only life trying to extend your life and miss living it in the process because that is all you focused on. There needs to be a balance, but again it's the ratio of that balance that is important.

High-H.I. living is where all you eat is junk which has been massively processed and interfered with. This is why a low-H.I way of life is the best of all worlds. You are simply looking for foods and drinks that have had some human intervention, but not enough to destroy the nutrients or to have added nasties which could cause you harm.

Here's a quick overview of the Low-H.I Way of Life. Once again, this is not set in stone, it's a guideline. It's up to you to ultimately design your own diet so that you are not on a diet.

The Low-H.I Way of Life

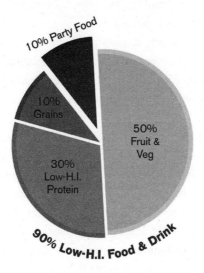

50% Should consist of high water content foods – such as fruits, vegetables (and their juices), soups and salads.

30% Can consist of proteins such as Low-H.I. fish, meat, nuts, seeds, etc.

10% Grains, such as rice and bread.

10% Party Food (High-H.I. foods and drinks).

Ninety per cent of the food and drink you consume each day should be low H.I. Of this 90 per cent, 50 per cent should be low-H.I., high water content foods such as fruits, vegetables (and their juices), soups and salads. 30 per cent should be proteins, such as Low-H.I. fish, meat, nuts, seeds, etc. And 10 per cent should be grains, such as rice and bread.

The remaining 10 per cent of your overall diet each day can be what I call 'party food' (i.e. High-H.I. food and drink). After following this programme, many people decide to avoid all High-H.I. food and drink because they feel so good.

Clearly you are not under an obligation to have 10 per cent High H.I. every day! But I have included this allowance for two reasons:

1 It is important to understand that the body can deal with a certain amount of anything without experiencing any weight gain or illness. I was extremely strict for many years and was, for want of a better phrase, a right royal pain in the arse (or ass for my American friends). Friends gave up inviting me for dinner as I was obsessed with food and was always trying to do the right thing. I wasn't eating any junk at all and was on a 100-per-cent Low-H.I diet 100 per cent of the time. I thought by not eating any junk I had removed my food problem, but all I had really done was to move it, not remove it.

2 That is not freedom. Freedom is about being free to design your own diet without becoming obsessed. We need to give our body some credit; it was designed to deal with a certain amount of anything. That certain amount, however, should be a maximum of 10 per cent of what you eat in a day.

We are human! And as humans we have dinner parties and, if we want a life with friends and family, we need to not be anal about food. Food is a fuel and it is vital that the vast majority of fuel coming into the body is the fuel designed to run it efficiently (Low-H.I living). At the same time, because we are human, it is also important to be free to have some High-H.I foods and drinks if the occasion calls for it. If your little one has made some cakes, you don't want to say, 'Sorry, I only eat Low-H.I.'! If you are having a romantic dinner overlooking the ocean, why not order a cheeky little dessert with two spoons to share? Personally most of the time I still don't eat High-H.I foods, but I'm no longer trapped in the 'never' mindset. I have the freedom to eat it when I want to – it's just that the vast majority of the time I don't want to because it doesn't satisfy me; instead it makes me want to eat more and makes me fat and miserable. But I can if I want to and that frees your mind and makes for a much freer life (so if you see me at an airport having a cheeky cappuccino, understand that I am human!)

Many will continue a juice-only way of life after the 5-day detox for a few more days or even 30. If that's you, and you are happy about doing it, then do it. The key, as I have done my best to communicate here, is you need to design your own diet based around the low H.I. way of life.

Clearly, you can do what you like; you can go and eat rubbish from here on in, but why would you want to? Just think how amazing you feel in the space of just five days of not having rubbish and getting some fresh juice inside you – why would you ever want to go back?

However, no matter what Low-H.I. or High-H.I. food you have, it is essential you adopt the second fundamental concept for long-term weight loss ...

THE
LAW
OF FOUR

Four Simple Rules For Life ... No Matter What You Eat!

16

1. ONLY EAT WHEN YOU ARE GENUINELY PHYSICALLY HUNGRY

This is an essential part of a permanently slim and healthy body. We often eat as a response to the clock or because of a habit, such as being on a plane or because it's noon. A great question to ask is, 'If I didn't know how much food I had eaten today, or what the time was – how hungry would I actually be?' Food of any kind will potentially store itself as fat if you eat when the body doesn't need fuel. The real pleasure in eating is when we end the empty, insecure feeling that is hunger. Not only do you not gain weight if you only eat when you're really hungry (when you also abide by the other rules here), but you also get more pleasure from the food you do eat.

Now that you have reached the end of the 5lbs in 5 Days programme you have cleared your body of all *false* hungers and you are in a position to recognize *genuine* hungers. Most people do in fact eat when they think they are genuinely hungry, but that is 'the Food Trick'. Junk food is designed to create *additional* hungers. These false hungers only seem to be satisfied by more junk, which is why often an apple just won't cut it.

2. EAT CONSCIOUSLY AND EAT SLOWLY – NO MATTER WHAT YOU ARE EATING!

Be aware of your eating, savour your food and take your time with it. This rule should apply no matter what you are eating, even if it's the odd bit of junk. Apart from eating too much of the wrong food, nothing – and I mean nothing – will cause weight gain more than the speed at which a person eats. Combine the two, i.e. eat too much food at 100 mile an hour, and it's the perfect recipe to pile the weight on in the fastest way possible. Often we are onto the next forkful before we have even swallowed the current one, so we miss the very experience we often crave anyway – eating.

I often hear people saying how much they love the experience of chocolate melting on their tongue slowly. SLOWLY! Most people shovel one chocolate in after the other. The enzymes in your saliva are more powerful than those in your stomach. By chewing your food thoroughly before swallowing, you not only make it much easier for your body to digest, but again you get to really enjoy your food.

So if you are going to eat a bit of rubbish, for whatever reason (we are all human and we do not want to ever play the perfection game, that's not what I am about), eat it slowly. If you are going to do it – enjoy it ... slowly. This is the one law I often have to talk to myself about as at times I can vacuum food down!

3. STOP EATING JUST BEFORE YOU ARE FULL AND USE THE 20-MINUTE RULE

Always finish eating before you are uncomfortably full and leave the table when you are still slightly hungry. Then wait 20 minutes. If you are still genuinely physically hungry, eat some more and do the same. However, you will find that if you do wait 20 minutes, you will not be hungry at all. Give your food a little time for the body to acknowledge its presence. This principle often doesn't apply when you eat 'empty foods' such as heavy refined-sugar-loaded products as they tend to raise sugars levels too high, and it's only when the hormone insulin is no longer in the bloodstream that we can feel satisfied. The body uses insulin to burn off excess sugar in the bloodstream. Insulin, so we are clear, is known as the 'fat-producing hormone'. This rule isn't always easy to do, but if you can train yourself to do it, it will make a massive difference long term.

4. KEEP HYDRATED!

Often when we are feeling hungry, the body in fact is crying out for water. Keep a bottle of water near you as often as possible and take regular sips. Fresh juices will keep you hydrated, but it's a good idea to sip water at regular intervals too. There are massive arguments over what kind of water we should be drinking and all have their merit. Personally I am more than happy to drink any mineral water.

★ ★ ★

The 'Law of Four' principles should be adopted no matter what you are eating, but these *laws* should defiantly be applied when not eating Low H.I.

Now you have the simple tools for life-long success, it's time to …

Be
LIMITLESS
AND MAKE
Your Life
EXTRAORDINARY

17

If you are reading this on Day 5, as requested, you should already be feeling a great deal better than when you started. If you haven't hit your 'juice high' just yet, don't panic – it's on its way! By the time you finish these five days you will have one of the most precious commodities you could wish for – momentum.

So the question is – where do you want to go from here? Do you want to go back to your old ways and end up in exactly the same situation you were in before? Or, do you want to take your health, your body and your life to the next level?

For many people a detox of this nature can be a 'Sliding Door' moment (as in the film). I have seen people go on to lose over 8 stone (112lbs – 50kg) after this Juice Master detox and completely transform their life. But at the same time I have also seen people go right back to where they started within a week of doing the detox. Which camp do you want to be in?

JUST ONCE!

Don't you want to get your health to where it's perhaps *never* been before and feel what it's like to have 'that body', even if it's just once in your life? Wouldn't you at least like to try it on for size? Wear what you want whenever you want? Not have to worry about how you look on a beach? Be in a position where you are running on full power most of the time? Wouldn't you like the energy to tap into your full potential in order to live the life you want on a daily basis? It's your shout clearly, but imagine if you continued with this lifestyle? Imagine what you would look like and how you would feel in a month if just five days has had this effect on you. Yes, there will be challenges along the way, but you will never be in a better position than right now to take your health, body and life to a place it may not have been for many years ... or even at all.

THE POWER OF MOMENTUM

One of the most precious commodities you can have is momentum. It's not always easy to get going, but once you build up enough momentum *everything* becomes just that little bit easier. Now you are on Day 5 you already have this very precious commodity and, if I were you, I'd do everything within my power to make sure I didn't lose it. The end of this full juice and exercise programme is a very unique time. You have lived on nothing but freshly extracted juice for five days and in doing so you have also had five full days without any *refined* fats, sugars, salts and other junk going into your body. You have also been doing at least an hour a day of SAB (Super After-burn) training; all of which creates tremendous momentum in the right direction. This momentum is extremely precious and the time to maximize its power is now!

You need to know momentum is always there and is just as powerful for good or for bad, which is why if you wish to take your body, life and health to another level you must utilize it now. For example, if you say to yourself that you're going to sit down for five minutes and watch a bit of TV, it will turn into an hour or even five. Equally if you go for a quick 5-minute run, it will turn into 30 or even 60 minutes. If you break the 'junk food' seal once one day; you'll do it twice the next day. If you eat well for a few days in a row, you have momentum and the chances are you will continue.

For some the end of the 5-day detox will be the end of it for them. They will feel and look a lot better than they did, but they won't look their *very* best. They won't get to that Holy Grail place, the place where they LOVE their body and feel on fire most of the time. They will gradually, but ever so surely, lose the momentum and go back to their old ways and BOOM! Before they know it, it's back to where they started.

There is nothing wrong with this, and I know many people who simply do either the 5- or 7-day juice diet about six times a year and just eat and drink anything in between. They use it as a 'service' for their body, or 're-charge' if you will, and they're more than happy to this.

But if you are really out of shape, and/or have many challenges with your health, why not use this as the biggest springboard you have ever had? You have a golden opportunity here to take this to a level you may never have done before, I mean *really* raise your game and get into über shape. You have the opportunity to really tap into and

harness the power of the momentum you currently have –
I hope you take it by the scruff of the neck and run with it.
If not now, then when?

BE LIMITLESS AND LET YOUR DREAMS PREVAIL

If you haven't seen it, *Limitless* is a film starring Bradley
Cooper (stop drooling!) who plays the main character Edward
'Eddie' Morra. Eddie is a New York City author suffering from
writer's block with a deadline looming and struggling after
being dumped by his girlfriend Lindy. One day, Eddie comes
across Vernon Gant, his ex brother-in-law. Vernon, a drug
dealer, offers Eddie a nootropic drug, NZT-48, claiming that
it was just approved by the FDA and that it allows the user
to access 100 per cent of his or her brain's capacity instead of
the 'usual' 20 per cent, thus giving them 'limitless' possibilities.
Eddie takes Vernon's card with his address and phone
number, accepts the pill and arrives home. He takes the pill
as he enters his apartment and finds it's true; with his
heightened brain activity, all of his senses become tuned in
to everything in his surrounding environment. He can recall
everything he has seen and heard, he can learn exponentially
faster, and he is able to outsmart and out-talk people. Taking
the pill transforms him from an uninspired, lethargic guy
who misses deadlines and can hardly make it through the
day to a superhuman who has *limitless* possibilities lying
before him. He goes from struggling to get a page done in a
fortnight, to being able to finish his manuscript in just a

week. He is transformed from a person who didn't want to get out of bed into someone who can't wait to jump out of bed with limitless energy and limitless possibilities. He even learns a language in a couple of days! Now clearly I am not suggesting for a second that living on juice for seven days will mean you'll be speaking Chinese by next weekend, but I feel the 'Limitless Pill' is a very good analogy as it often describes perfectly how some people feel by the morning of Day 6. On Day 5 of one of our Global Juice Detoxes we had a post on our Facebook page that read,

> Day 5 and feeling AMAZING … lost 5lbs, have crazy energy!
> Not hungry at all, even forgot to drink one of my juices yesterday!
> **It feels like I'm on some magic pill …** but it's just juice …

Another one read,

> **… the only way I can aptly describe it is like being in an old black and white film and suddenly jumping over to colour!**

And that really does capture the feeling for many people – it's like going from black and white to colour.

When you remove all of the toxicity (refined sugars, fats, etc.) coming in, replace the deficiencies (vitamins, minerals, amino acids, essential fatty acids, phytonutrients, enzymes, etc.) and do some exercise, the 'fuzzy head' syndrome lifts and you start to feel on fire again, or 'limitless'. It's not until you live for at least five days without *any* rubbish coming into the body, while furnishing your system with the essential nutrients it craves, that you start to fully realize just how much the wrong foods and drinks affect your life.

The reason I have added this mini chapter to the book and asked specifically you read it on Day 5, is purely because I don't want you to lose one of the most valuable commodities you can have – *momentum*. I don't want you to lose this 'limitless' feeling and not to tap into the possibilities that lie before you. I don't want you to lose the 'colour', if you will. Even if I only get to one of you and you go on to get *that* body and tap into a level of living and potential which may have passed you by till now, then it's more than been worth it.

FULLY RECHARGED!

If there is any time in your life you are going to make a major *real permanent* change then this really is it. I cannot stress enough what an opportunity lies before you right now and how important it is to harness this momentum. You need to understand that this 're-charge' only lasts a certain amount of time and it's different for everyone, which is why it's so important to allow your limitless possibilities to shine now. Personally I need a 're-charge' every couple of months to keep my goals on track and to take my life to the level I want it to consistently be. We *all* run out of gas, as life is life, and we all need to plug ourselves in from time to time. So while you feel fired up, raise your game and by the time you reach the need for your next 're-charge', you will already be starting from a new higher level. We all drop slightly from time to time and no one is perfect, nor should we ever play the perfection game, but each time you 're-charge' you have the potential to take your body, health and life to a new level. This means every time you drop back slightly you are still at a better level than before you started. Take a look at this Facebook post which illustrates what I mean:

> This is the third time of doing this programme. 18 months ago I decided that enough was enough and started on the 7lbs in 7 days and lost 10lbs, went onto Turbo Charge and lost 3st (42lbs), my life changed completely and I thought I had my diet under control. Then the food I ate started to change until I found I had gained back nearly a stone! So doing this has really helped, it has kick started me back on the road to healthy eating. Jason, thank you so very much for your passion and encouragement. Just weighed and lost 10.5lbs. 'Nothing tastes as good as being healthy feels', I have this mantra in my head now. Thank you to everyone.
>
> *Jackie*

Jackie lost 3 stone (42lbs) and then gained almost 14lbs over time. She recognized what was happening, 're-charged' herself and lost 10.5lbs in a week, and will easily end up, not only on track, but *above* where she fell back to.

I urge each and every one of you to really run with this, follow the principles laid out in the Low-H.I. Way Of Life and 'just once' get the body and health you ultimately crave.

LET'S JUICE THE WORLD TOGETHER

Thank you for taking the time to read the book and do the programme. My mission is to 'Juice the World', which is hard to do all alone. Please spread the juicy word and help inspire others about the juicy side of life. If you want to find me I'm on Twitter @juicemaster and on Facebook: 'Jason Vale Juice Master'.

I started the book with stories I hoped would inspire you to complete the 5-day juice detox. I will leave you with some truly breathtaking stories which I hope will inspire you to your ultimate goal. Please make a point of reading them. If I don't ever get the opportunity to meet you personally, have an extraordinary life and …

May the Juice Be with You!

INSPIRED
FOR
LIFE!

18

I LOST 7.5 STONE AND CURED MY DIABETES!

I have been called fat all my life, Last year I turned 50 and I weighed 21.5 stone (301lbs/136kg). I'd just had an exploratory operation on my knee and was told there was a good chance within the next few years I would need a knee replacement. My type 2 diabetes was so far out of control that tablets were no longer doing the job and the next move was injecting. I was on 6 types of medication, did no real exercise, ate a lot of junk food and drank a lot of diet coke and beer! I knew I had to change so I read Slim For Life and IT WAS LIFE CHANGING. Today thanks to juicing, I am 14 stone (105lbs/48kg lost), only on one medication that I will soon be off, no longer have diabetes, go to the gym at least 3 days a week, cycle 20 miles a week and walk my dog 2-4 miles every day. THANK YOU!

Anthony

I'VE LOST 42LBS AND CLEARED MY PSORIASIS!

I have lost 42lbs since January! My cholesterol is now normal, my blood sugar levels are great, my blood pressure is now perfect and I look and feel better than I have felt in years. Since January, along with the 42lbs of excess weight, I have also cleared all my psoriasis! I have also gone from 300mg of Thyroxin to just 50mg and I have also lost a whole host of other complaints including Irritable Bowel Syndrome, bloating, cramping, constipation and diarrhoea. It really feels like I have healed myself. My diet is now very much based on fruit and vegetables with meat and fish very occasionally, all in smaller quantities than before. The combination of no wheat, dairy and a plentiful supply of fruit and veggie-based juices has just made an amazing difference to me. THANK YOU, THANK YOU, THANK YOU!

Carolyn

MY MOTHER AND I HAVE BOTH LOST 8 STONE (112LBS)

My mum was very poorly last year suffering with tiredness, fatigue and terrible migraines which would floor her for days. She had no energy, and something had to change. Meanwhile, I ended up with gall stones after an extremely stressful birth with my third child, and as I was into alternative therapy, I read that juicing would help, so I bought the book 7lbs in 7 days and thought –

this is it, Mum and I have to follow this! In August last year we embarked on the 7-day juicing programme. Mum's start weight was 15+ stone (210lbs +) and in that one week she lost a whole stone (14lbs) in weight! We then read midweek Turbo Charge Your Life in 14 Days and have stuck to this ever since. Mum is now a size 12 (UK) and just under 11 stone (154lbs), and I'm now a size 8 (UK) and weigh 9 stone 3 (130lbs) and we couldn't be happier! Mum has bundles of energy and I do yoga – we are both so, so happy! THANK YOU!

I'VE LOST 50LBS WHICH THEN INSPIRED MY SON TO LOSE 60LBS!

Juicing has changed my life in a sense that I feel like I can conquer the world. I have no health insurance and it has really given me that piece of mind to know that I can be as healthy as I can be, not only for myself but also as a type of legacy that I am passing down to my children. My results were amazing to say the least. I have lost a total of 50lbs since I began. My son (who is 25) has also been inspired and he has seen amazing results as well. He has lost almost 60lbs since Aug 2013 and looks amazing. It helps when you have a buddy. I didn't follow any specific programme, I just started juicing. I juiced a combination of fruits for breakfast and then a 'green' juice for lunch. I mostly juiced the produce that was on sale at my local supermarket for budget reasons. I then felt because I was nutritionally satisfied from the day I could make better choices for snacks and dinner.

I LOST 28LBS AND DROPPED FROM 21 PER CENT BODY FAT TO 12.5 PER CENT, ALL THANKS TO JUICING!

I got into juicing just before Christmas 2012 when a friend gave me their old juicer along with Jason Vale's book to try out. I started reading the book and it all seemed so simple and logical that I decided to give it a go! I signed up to the 'World Biggest Juice Detox' and did Jason's 7-day juice programme with my wife. We both felt amazing at the end of the week so decided to do the detox every quarter! The rest of the time, we juice for breakfast, juice or salad for lunch and then normal, healthy dinner! By June I was on top form for my big race City to Summit triathlon in Scotland – and I am confident that juicing paid a big part in getting me sharp for race day as well as providing me with a natural sports drink on race day itself. I can tell you, no doubt – I was flying! **I lost 2 stone (28lbs)** in weight, I went from 13 stone (182lbs) to 11 (154lbs) and **my body fat dropped from 21 per cent to 12.5 per cent.** My health is massively improved – **I have clearer skin, improved hay fever and asthma and I am more alert and alive than ever before!** Plus, I look much more toned and my run/bike times have dramatically improved by shedding the extra pounds! Great results all round, THANK YOU!

Luke

I DROPPED 91LBS, CAME OFF DEPRESSION MEDS AND BECAME A BETTER DAD

I bought Jason Vale's 7lbs in 7 days app. I have used it over the past two years, using all the juices from the app and now mixing my own fruits and veg recipes. **I stopped drinking, came off all my depression medication, got back into playing the sports that I loved when I was younger and to top it off, I lost 91lbs!** I now live a completely different lifestyle. **I am the happiest, healthiest person I have ever been.** I was drinking, gambling and making all the wrong choices in life, now I am living a clean lifestyle and have more energy than I have ever had. My anger issues are resolved more easily and I am in a great relationship now. I've tried different diets in the past, which in the short term I lost a few pounds on, however I always gained it back. I love juicing because unlike other diets, I have maximum energy, my skin glows and I have so much confidence. Like Jason says, juicing is not a diet, it is a lifestyle. **What motivates me to stick to my new lifestyle is how well I feel about myself and what a better parent I am now to my son.** I'm always running around playing with him, which I couldn't before when I was 291lbs. Wanting to be a better father was probably my biggest motivation, it also keeps me motivated hearing all the compliments on how good I look now.

Ryan

I LOST 6 STONE (84LBS) AND CURED MY ASTHMA, ECZEMA AND IBS THROUGH JUICING

I was obese and I had epilepsy, asthma, eczema and IBS, and my children were living on the same junk food as me. I discovered that I was also anaemic and was very tired all the time. Then about four years ago, I started looking into juicing. I read some articles in magazines and online, and wondered if it really could work for me. I had very little confidence though, and was convinced it wouldn't. However, I decided to order the book and DVD of 7lbs in 7 days to find out more. That was a life-changing moment for me. Reading and watching Jason and the way he explains the psychology of eating really got me thinking. It was the first time I'd read anything like that, and it really changed the way I looked at my diet and my life. So I saved up and bought myself a juicer and a rebounder. It's one of the best decisions I've ever made. I'm happier and healthier, and finally in control. Every morning I get up early, do yoga and then start juicing. I now have more confidence to do the things I want to do in my life. I'm slimmer, healthier and much more focused on my goals. **I no longer have asthma, eczema or IBS. My iron levels have increased and I'm no longer anaemic** and in January this year, **I came off epilepsy medication after being on them for 21 years.** I have **lost 6 stones (84lbs)** altogether, and **gone from a size 18-20 to 8-10.** Even more importantly though, I now feel that anything is possible, and that I can make my dreams happen. It took a lot of courage, but I attended Jason's Juice Academy this year and it was an amazing experience, one that I'll never forget. My children also have juices everyday, and really love them. They are very healthy and do lots of sports. My dream is to help and inspire other people to, not only change their diets, but their lives too because I now know it's possible.

Kelly

There are thousands of these. I can't put them all in … But I will leave you with this very lovely email. If this doesn't inspire anyone – nothing will …

I just wanted to send a 'little' message with HUGE THANKS to Jason. Eight months ago I weighed 17.5 stone (245lbs) the heaviest I'd ever weighed. I think I would have just carried on getting bigger and more unfit. I had a wake-up call as my health started to suffer – I was finding it hard to breathe after walking down the road and I started wheezing. I also was at an all-time low confidence-wise – luckily I've always had a very supportive husband and daughters. Well, I decided to go to my doctor as I really thought my health was suffering. She was very good; she listened to me and my chest and she prescribed me an inhaler and those tablets that bind fat.

Well, I took them for a month then found your books. Something clicked in my head. You made such sense. From that point on I bought a juicer which came with your recipe book. I told myself it was an investment in me and my health – well, that certainly is an understatement!! I decided I wanted to be healthy and slim, not just slim – cutting down on all the 'good' stuff as I'd done before lost the weight, but then I put it all back on as I hadn't changed my attitude to food.

I do think attitude is the key to changing bad habits – if you can do that you are half way there. I'd never put the health of my body first before – I just wanted to lose weight. So I stopped taking the tablets after talking to my doctor. I told her about juicing and that I didn't want to have to use an inhaler. She kindly agreed to weigh me every month (I don't have scales in the house as before I've always jumped on them every time I went past). Well, I am soooo proud to say that I'm **8 months on and have lost 7 stone (98lbs). I can't begin to say just how fantastic I feel both in body and mind – I don't wheeze, snore or get out of breath,** unless running for the bus, ha ha! It seemed very daunting knowing I had to lose 8 stone. I still have a stone to lose but I'm in **my BMI range – it was 44, now it is 24.8. How cool is that?** It's good to notice the little exciting things, like being able to fit in a plane seat and buckle up without bashing the next person and buying clothes from any shop. My doctor gets as excited as me every time I lose weight, which really pushes me on …

Well, sorry for such a long message – I did say it was going to be little, ha ha! Just want to say thank you for being my inspiration – I've gone on to look at other good websites and have learned such a lot but you were the one that started me off and as they say, the first step is the hardest. I'm telling anyone who will listen about juicing and its fantastic benefits.

Take care and thank you again from one happy Lynn.

PS: My advice to anyone thinking about juicing and becoming healthy would be to just do it! I wrote a disadvantage list and advantage list of losing weight – I had about 20 things on the advantage list and only one on the disadvantage and it was not being able to eat everything, anytime. Well, that is how a diet makes you feel – if you ration 'nice' foods you crave them more, but if you view food differently and put your body first and think of it as the only one you'll have, so nourish it and it will take care of you, you don't see 'nice' food as a treat or to be craved after, you see juicy melon, strawberries, juices etc. as nourishing clean foods that will enable your body to function at its best for as long as it can. I now really crave tomatoes – can't get enough of them. My husband said he was going to buy me a tomato plant instead of flowers for my birthday – how cool is that? I said I'd love it – he thought I was joking, but I wasn't – he couldn't give me a nicer present. Just lastly, if I, a Choco/ Crispo/ foodaholic of 20 years, can change, so can anyone.

THE
Q & A
Section

19

Q: WHAT DETOX SYMPTOMS SHOULD I EXPECT?

A: This depends on the individual, everyone reacts differently. Some people have no noticeable detox symptoms and just crack on with their lives, while some really feel it. The main physical symptoms are headaches, tiredness and for some, anxiety. The reason for these is not so much due to actual detox but down to withdrawal. Refined sugars and fats are extremely addictive, and like many addictive substances, withdrawal can cause tiredness, headaches and anxiety. If you are in the right frame of mind (please read 'Mind over Fatter!', pp. 93–107) then the chances are that you will barely notice any adverse physical symptoms. However, even if you do, know they are very temporary and should last a maximum of 72 hours. If you are usually a very heavy caffeine drinker or refined sugar head, then the chances of you experiencing more headaches and tiredness are naturally increased as the body goes through the withdrawal. Please though don't make the mistake of thinking everything you experience for the five days you are on this detox are because you are on the detox. There will be many times in your life when you haven't been on a detox and experienced tiredness during the day, for example. You don't put it down to anything in particular; you just feel tired and assume you've been working too hard or haven't had enough sleep. However, the second people experience the same thing when on the juice detox it's *because* you are on it. In a normal week you will experience a range of different levels of tiredness, anxiety, hunger, stress and may even get the odd headache. So the chances of experiencing any of these when on a detox week are high, as we get them anyway! Yes, what you may experience might indeed be down to the withdrawal or detox, but then it might just be what you usually experience from time to time. If you do experience any adverse feelings, drink some water and get some rest if you are able to. What is important is not to overanalyse whatever detox symptoms you may or may not experience. They are a very small price to pay for how you will feel when you come out the other side.

Q: WILL I BE GETTING ENOUGH CALORIES?

A: Yes. It is just five days and even if you were to have nothing but water, you'd still be OK. Personally I am not a calorie man as, like so many aspects of the health and nutrition world, looking at calories in food has many flaws. I would rather look at the level of genuine nutrition in a food than worry about whether it meets my RDA (Recommended Daily Allowance) of calories. I could hit my RDA by having a fry-up for breakfast and a burger and fries for dinner, but how much genuine nutrition is there in that? It's not our calorie 'needs' we should be focusing on, but rather our nutritional needs; the two are simply not the same.

We also need to acknowledge that the RDA of calories is made up. Our personal daily allowance of anything is just that – personal. It depends on what you are doing on a particular day (physically and mentally); your muscle mass; your age and a billion other variables. The nutritional powers that be say that the average man needs around 2,500 calories a day to maintain his weight, and the average woman needs about 2,000 calories a day. All I know is this; if I eat 2,500 calories of refined fat and sugar for days on end and do no exercise, I gain weight. If I eat 2,500 calories of plant food and fish, I don't! Please don't get caught up in the calorie madness and just trust you will be getting enough *nutrition* for the five days you are on this detox.

Q: SHOULD I BRUSH MY TEETH AFTER EACH JUICE?

A: No. If you do, you brush away your teeth's natural protective layer, so wait at least an hour before brushing your teeth. If you are nervous about juices and your teeth at all then use a large straw. Once again though, the main reason juices have a bad name when it comes to teeth is because of mass market 'cooked' juices, which can be like sugar, as opposed to 'live' freshly extracted vegetable-based juices.

Q: WHAT TOILET MOVEMENTS SHOULD I EXPECT?

A: Some people go less than usual and others more; both are nothing to worry about. Many people don't really notice their toilet movements on a day-to-day basis, but the second they're on a detox, they start to be concerned. Even if you don't go at all during the five days, providing you aren't in pain in that area, don't worry as the second you start eating

Low H.I. Foods you'll be good. Personally I have no issue on this front when doing this particular plan as it has plenty of soluble and insoluble fibre, but if you do, don't worry!

Q: SHOULD I HAVE A COLONIC BEFORE I START?

A: This is a very personal choice and there is no need to do so, but you may *want* to do so. The science is not conclusive when it comes to colonics, but then science isn't everything. I know many people who swear by them and I am not adverse to them myself. My take is this; if you have eaten extremely badly for many months or years, then having a colonic before you start isn't a bad idea. When I filmed my documentary *Super Juice Me!* I ate very badly before it (it was part of a larger experiment) and so made sure I had a colonic a week when I did the month of juice only. If nothing else, it makes you feel immediately lighter and hydrates your body like nothing else. Some people choose to have a colonic every day during the detox, others just one before they start and most don't have one at all. The point is, providing you go to a good colonic hydro therapist, it won't do any harm. It does remove some good bacteria so you'd need to take a few capsules after it. Colonics are something we do offer at our Juicy Oasis retreat and many people do swear by them. If you don't have one, don't panic as the body is perfectly equipped to keep you moving!

Q: HOW LONG WILL MY JUICES LAST ONCE MADE?

A: This all depends on what juicer you have made them in and how they have been stored. If you make all your juices in a slow juicer (masticating) then, providing it is immediately stored into a thermos flask or bottle of some kind which blocks all light and oxygen, then you'll be good for three days. Even if the bottles are clear, as long as they are in the fridge, no light will be getting to them. If you juice in a normal fast juicer, like the Philips, then because it creates more heat friction than a slow juicer, the juice only lasts for a day (unless you freeze it – see next question), providing you still store it away from light and oxygen. You cannot beat juice freshly made and drunk within the first 10 minutes, but I know life doesn't always allow that. I know people who bring their juicer to work; now that's commitment, but for many storing in a flask is all good.

Q: I DON'T HAVE TIME TO JUICE FOUR TIMES A DAY – CAN I FREEZE THEM?

A: The simple answer is yes. When you freeze juice you lose very little of the nutrient content; this is in massive contrast to when you apply heat to fresh juice, which can destroy the vast majority of vitamin and enzyme (life) content. Virtually all shop-bought juices have been pasteurized, or 'cooked' if you prefer, at high temperatures, which is why bottled juices are in no way shape or form a replacement for making them fresh at home. Once made you can add to a BPA-free water bottle (remembering to leave a little room spare for freezing expansion) and pop in the freezer. Once frozen, take out the night before and place in the fridge for the next day. Remove about an hour before you want to drink the juice. Freezing is a practice we use in our www.juicemasterdelivered.com service and is the perfect next best thing. If you can make fresh though, it is always the preferred method as you still have to take into account the defrosting time, which can lower the nutrient content.

Q: I CAN'T EXERCISE, WILL THE JUICES ALONE BE ENOUGH TO SUCCEED?

A: Yes. If you don't do any exercise at all and simply drink the juices, then you should indeed still drop 5lbs in 5 days and feel amazing. However, if you follow the SAB training (page 133) then you take it to a whole new level. I wholeheartedly advise doing exercise as well as the plan. If the SAB is too intense for your needs, then yoga and rebounding are wonderful exercise tools.

Q: WHERE WILL I GET MY PROTEIN AND CALCIUM?

A: I have covered this in the main body of text in the book, but in case you skipped it, here's my take again. The largest land animals on earth are vegan. Giraffes, rhinos, elephants, hippos, bullocks and some other large animals eat no meat and drink no milk at all. They build all their muscle and bone mass through plant food. Protein is built from amino acids, the building blocks for protein. On this programme you will be getting enough amino acids and calcium through the juices and your Hunger SOS. It is only five days and even if plant food provided no protein or calcium, you would still not have either a protein or a calcium deficiency in that short space of time.

It is always interesting to observe how people are concerned about a lack of certain nutrients when stopping junk food and going onto fresh juice. I am unsure if they were ever concerned about their protein, calcium and other nutrient intake when they were eating and drinking junk, but for some reason the second they start healthy drinking and eating these irrational concerns come into play. This is largely due to the amount of conditioning we have had since birth from the meat and milk marketing boards. I have written enough about this in other books, but please do not worry – you will be getting the right nutrients during the five days on freshly extracted juice.

Q: IS IT SAFE TO DO THE PROGRAMME IF PREGNANT?

A: Clearly, with anything like this, always check with your GP or medical practitioner first. Right, now that's out of the way, here are my personal views. I cannot see why, unless you are allergic to a specific fruit or vegetable in the programme, you wouldn't be able to do this while pregnant. Many of the fruits and vegetables in this programme contain folic acid (folate) beta-carotene, vitamin C and potassium. Beta-carotene is needed for your baby's cell and tissue development, vision, and immune system. The vitamin C is crucial for your baby's bones and teeth, as well as the collagen in your baby's connective tissue. The potassium helps control blood pressure, and folic acid helps prevent neural tube defects and promotes a healthy birth weight. There is almost an entire book that could be written on why many of the fruits and vegetables found in this 5-day programme are not only *safe* but *essential* for an expecting mother to take. However, because this is a 'juice only' programme, and as such not recognized by the powers-that-be as being as good as the whole food, you need to contact your GP first. Please remember that it's only the juice contained within the fibres that feed the body; fibre does not penetrate through the intestinal wall, making this condensed form of nutrition every bit as nutritious as the whole food.

Q: CAN I DRINK TEA, COFFEE OR ALCOHOL WHILE ON THE PROGRAMME?

A: You can have as many herbal teas as you like, but no 'normal' tea, coffee or alcohol should be consumed on the programme. It is a detox after all, not a retox. If you are desperate for something containing caffeine, then Green Tea may be drunk in moderation while on this programme. Green Tea is not only a wonderful source of antioxidants and good plant chemicals, but can induce thermo-genesis and stimulate fat oxidation, boosting the metabolic rate 4 per cent without increasing the heart rate.

Q: I'M NOT DRINKING ALL OF THE JUICES – DOES IT MATTER?

A: Ideally you shouldn't skip any of the juices as the programme has been carefully designed to make sure you get a *spectrum of nutrition* every day. However, during the test phase of this programme, some people mentioned that on a couple of occasions through the week they simply didn't feel like their juice and opted for their HUNGER SOS instead. This is perfectly OK and you should always listen to your body and not 'force' juice down. However, one of the key reasons why it is important to have your juice at the times allocated is to make sure your sugar levels don't drop to an uncomfortable level. If this happens it could cause you to look for a quick sugar fix, and ultimately to knock the plan on the head. The morning and evening juices are the ones not to avoid as they are the thick ones designed to keep you satiated.

Q: I DON'T HAVE A JUICER – CAN I JUST USE MY BLENDER?

A: NO! and in case you missed it – NO. A juicer extracts the juice contained within the fibres and a blender simply blends the fibres and the juice together. The idea behind juicing is rapid nutrition; removing the insoluble fibres so that the juice can be readily absorbed and nutrition be more bio-available to the cells. If you stick everything in a blender you end up with an extremely thick concoction, which, ironically, is difficult to digest, and, more importantly, extremely difficult for the body to fully utilize. It is not so much that you are what you eat, but rather you are what you manage to absorb and with all that insoluble fibre going into the stomach at once, absorption becomes that much more difficult. The most I add to the blender at any one time is either a banana, an avocado, a little yoghurt or a few nuts and seeds. What you will never see me doing is adding in stacks of whole fruits and vegetables, a load of nuts, blending it all together and then drinking it in 10 seconds flat – as many people do. This is not good for you! Things like avocados do not juice so they have to be blended, but anything that can be juiced, I juice. If you are going to do this juice plan then you will need a juicer and a blender – you cannot do this plan with just a blender. Well you can, but you will feel bloated, the drinks will suck and you'll throw in the towel – so if you don't have one, time to get the best investment you'll ever make for your health, a good juicer. (See Chapter 20, So Which Juicer Is Best, Jase?, Page 255.)

Q: I'M ALLERGIC/INTOLERANT TO A CERTAIN FRUIT OR VEGETABLE IN THE PROGRAMME – CAN I ADJUST?

A: Yes. Please feel free to adjust the plan if you have a genuine allergy to any of the ingredients in the programme. I say 'genuine' as many people are under the false impression they are allergic or intolerant to certain foods when they aren't at all. If you are genuinely allergic then clearly avoid whatever it is you are allergic to, but if you have been told you are intolerant to a certain food, don't just go along with it. Food intolerance tests are everywhere, and from my experience you can go from one to the other all day long and get conflicting results on what foods you should avoid. If these tests were 100 per cent accurate then you should score the same no matter where you go, but this is rarely the case.

There are of course genuine cases of people being allergic to certain fruit and vegetables, but it is rare for most. I had someone at my retreat once say they were allergic to apples. This was a little bit of an issue as ALL the juices at the 'juice only' juice retreat had apple in them. I said it wasn't a problem – I would make all of their juices with carrot instead as a base. Within two days they asked for the apple-based ones to test as a) they thought they would taste better (which clearly they do) and b) they couldn't actually remember the last time they'd had an adverse reaction to apples – they had just been told at a food-testing clinic that they were allergic to them. Needless to say, they drank the apple-based juices for the next five days and were fine.

Having said all that, if you do need to replace a fruit and veg, then please do – but try to replace it with a similar thing. If apples don't agree with you, replace them with pears, for example. If avocados don't agree with you, replace them with bananas – BUT you will also need to add some essential fatty acids in the form of Omega-3/6/9 oil to the blender. The avocados are there to make sure you get the right fats and if you pull these out you need to add the oil. Udo's Oil is a very good source, but supermarkets and health shops stock many different brands.

Q: DO I NEED ANY SUPPLEMENTS WHILE ON THE PLAN?

A: The answer is no ... but. The 'but' is there to cover all bases. You will not need any further supplementation if you buy good-quality fruit and vegetables. I know that in my last programme, the 7lbs in 7 Days Juice Master Diet, some people weren't happy with having to buy extra supplements, even though they were optional. I added them in to make sure that even if someone didn't buy the best quality fruit or veg, they would still get the finest quality super plant nutrition through the supplements.

If you have the app you will have seen that I make up a Power Greens drink by adding a dried green juice powder supplement to water. This is something we have every day at my retreats before we work out and it's something I would highly recommend, but clearly it's optional. If you have wonderful quality fruit and veg then no worries, just do the programme as is with the right produce. If you want to raise the game slightly on the nutrition front, get some Juice Master Power Greens or similar (as many places sell green powders these days, just be careful though as some have fillers and are not always the best quality).

There will of course be some who feel I am simply trying to sell supplements and if you are one of those cynical people, then just buy from someone else or leave them out. All I know is I spent over a year developing the finest dried green juice powders and they are something I have used myself for many years. I would also highly recommend some good quality friendly bacteria. This is not those silly little bottles of yoghurt, which are often loaded with sweeteners, but rather good quality capsules or live powder.

Q: HOW MUCH WEIGHT CAN I EXPECT TO LOSE?

A: Although the average person will lose between 5lbs–7lbs in five days on the programme, this is not the case for everyone. There are some people who will drop more and others will lose less. There can be many reasons for both, but here are the main ones:

1 If you are very overweight to start with the chances are that you will lose more weight than if you start at your ideal weight or close to it. There have been cases where people have lost as much as 10lbs in just five days. But in cases where there is such dramatic weight loss it's usually because the person had quite a lot to lose to start with. There are cases where people have lost that amount even when close to their ideal weight to start with, but it's rare.

2 There have been cases where people stick to the programme religiously and yet don't lose a great deal of weight during the five days. Often the reason for this is 'lag time'. Many people make the mistake of binging on disproportionate amounts of fat, sugar and salt a few days before the plan. This, on its own, would normally cause weight gain in the days following. However, because the person then removes all refined sugars, fats and salts and has a 100 per cent plant-based diet, no weight gain is experienced, but no weight is lost either. The person then can lose faith in the juice programme, believing the juice detox isn't working, when in fact it's working perfectly well but will take a little longer to see the results. In some cases it can take a few days after the programme to finish as 'lag time' works both ways. If you are not experiencing weight loss in the first 3–4 days and recognize that you may have overeaten more than usual in the days leading up to the juice detox, have faith and carry on; it will work.

Q: CAN I DO THIS PROGRAMME WHILE ON MEDICATION?

A: You must *always* consult your doctor first as there are some juices which can affect certain medical drugs. Having said this, this is very rare and in most cases it is more than safe to do this programme while on medication, but always talk to your GP first.

Q: I KNOW YOU AREN'T A FAN OF MEDICAL DRUGS SO SHOULD I NOT USE ANY WHILE ON THE PROGRAMME?

A: Let me be very clear on this one. Short-term medical intervention is *very* necessary at times and in some cases, long-term medical drug use is also necessary. There is no question however that we are taking far too many pills unnecessarily and over far too long periods of time. This is a separate book in itself, but for the purposes of this question, do not come off any medical drugs unless instructed to do so by your GP. If you are taking OCDs (Over the Counter Drugs) then it's your choice, but I would skip headache tablets and the like and allow the body to have pure natural goodness for the five days.

So Which *JUICER* Is Best, Jase?

20

Not the easiest question to answer any more,
but here goes ...

THE JUICER REVOLUTION

If there was a list of the top ten questions I get asked most frequently, then 'What juicer should I get?' is probably at number one, with 'But what about the fibre?' and 'Isn't it all just sugar?' coming in strongly at numbers two and three. The answer to the number one question used to be easy, but times have changed and the juicer market is as swamped and confusing as most other markets.

When I first set out on my mission to 'Juice the World', over 15 years ago now, the range of juice extractors was hardly long – in fact, it is safe to say it was pretty non-existent. If, and it was a very big *if*, you could find a juicer for sale in a regular electrical store (internet shopping hadn't really started at this time, and even if you did find anything you wanted to buy on the www, people just didn't trust giving their credit card details – my, how things have changed), all you would have found was an extremely cheap, flimsy, small juicer. It would have had a tiny kidney-shaped feeder for your fruits and vegetables and an extremely small pulp container. You would have had to chop all your fruit and veg into extremely small pieces and spend an age making a juice. If you wanted to make juice for a few of you, forget it; the machine would often block after making a single juice. You then would have had all the fun of the fair cleaning the thing, which was no easy task. Back then, of course, the people who manufactured juicers hadn't thought about how long it may take someone to clean it. Actually, they hadn't really thought about the juicing process as a whole! This was probably due to the market being so tiny; not even 1 per cent of the UK, for example, owned a juicer at that time. My mission was, and still is today, to make a juicer and blender as common as a kettle and toaster in every kitchen globally. This goal is not that far off, as juicers and blenders are now commonplace and I like to think I may have had a little something to do with this. However, the point I am making is that back then I used to tell people to just 'get a juicer'; now of course it's all about 'Yes, but which one?'

Luckily juicing has moved on from the nightmare of juicers past and 21st-century juicing is here to stay. Like most things in our fast-paced modern world, speed is key for a lot of people. Juice extractors have essentially gone 'broadband' and the vast majority now come with a wide chute, which usually allows for two or three apples to be juiced whole – no chopping, no peeling, no hassle! This is something I dreamt of when I first started juicing. However, not all wide-funnel juicers are built the same. There are many coming in 'off the shelf' from places like Asia, and big companies are simply adding their name to, often inferior, juicers. Many are very poorly made and lack the ability to actually juice. Yes, you can *get* juice from them, but often the pulp contains as much juice as the juice itself. When you buy a juice extractor you need a machine that does 'exactly what it says on the tin' (so to speak), i.e. *extract* the *juice* efficiently from the fibres.

AND THE BEST JUICER IN THE WORLD IS ...?

This is not the easiest question to answer because the best juicer in the world hasn't even been invented yet. As I have mentioned, I have been juicing for over 15 years and I have seen some great strides in juicing machines, but I have yet to find that elusive 'self-cleaning juicer'! This is the holy grail of juicers, and although we may be quite a way from an automatic self-cleaning juicer, I have good intelligence informing me that the 'semi-self-cleaning juicer' is just around the corner. By the time you read this book, 'one-click, semi-self-cleaning' technology may be here, and if so, I would say this is probably the juicer you want to get, especially if this is your first outing to the juicing world. If it's not out yet, or the rumours were just that – rumours – then the best juicer to get is simple. In my first ever book I set out what the best exercise in the world is, and the answer is: *the one you will do*. The same is now true of juicers. The best juicer in world is quite simply the one *you* will use, the one that suits *your* needs and, because looks do matter, the one that you feel will look coolest in your kitchen!

Currently there are three types of juicer to choose from:

Fast (centrifugal)
Slow (cold press or masticating)
Low-induction

Fast Juicers

These are by far the most common types of juicer on the market. Fast juicers, or 'centrifugal' juicers, as they are otherwise known, make up the vast majority of juicers sold in the world today. Most have very wide chutes, meaning you can put whole apples in, and they are extremely fast at juicing. There isn't a great deal to choose from these days in terms of performance, but you do tend to get what you pay for – I call it being 'reassuringly priced'. If you see a wide-funnel juicer at £40, there's usually a good reason it's just £40. We tend to spend a great deal of money on nights out, pay-per-view TV, alcohol, junk food and so on, but the second you ask someone to invest decent money in a juicer – something that can potentially help them live a long and disease-free existence – cries of 'That's too expensive!' soon follow. I used to buy two to three packets of cigarettes a day; at today's prices, that's over £20 … *a day!* If I had smoked for 40 years of my life it would amount to over £300,000. The average person in the UK spends over £140,000 in their lifetime on alcohol, and £2,620 a year on takeaways. People aged between 25 and 34 are the biggest consumers of fast food, spending over £200 a month on the stuff (over 24 takeaways a month). Once you start to look at the numbers, which don't even take into account the money spent on medication to treat many of the health conditions these things often spawn, the investment in a juicer and blender starts to look very attractive indeed! Fast juicers are not only the most common, but the best value too. This is why, especially if this is your first introduction to juicing, I would say this is the type of juicer you want to get. They are the easiest to use, the quickest, the easiest to clean and now they even look cool too. Even the top players in this field, at the time of writing this – Philips, Sage and Retro – will all set you back less than £200. The **Retro Super Fast Juicer** is the newest of all these and not only does it look as cool as hell, it's also super fast to use and to clean! I would also say, at this time, the **Retro Super Fast** Juicer is always best value for what you get in this sector (**www.retrojuicer.com**). However, like mobile phones or any other technology, the juice extractor market is always changing and new innovations are coming in thick and fast, so check out **www. juicemaster.com** for my up-to-date recommendations.

Slow Juicers

Slow juicers are also known as 'masticating' or 'cold press' juicers and tend to be more expensive and, as the name suggests, slower to use. However, when it comes to price, again, you tend to get what you pay for. Even though they cost more, the quality of the juice is quite literally out of this world. Slow juicers extract the juice at *much* slower speeds and therefore don't create the heat friction that many fast juicers do. The pulp left behind is also often bone dry, meaning that if you are going to juice a lot, you'll save money on produce as more of the juice is extracted and not left in the pulp container. Having said that, there are now slow juicers that have whole chutes, meaning you can put whole apples in, making the process of 'cold press' juicing slightly faster. I say 'slightly' because even with a whole chute for apples, many still only move at 65–150 rpms, so will always be much slower than the 15,000 rpm fast juicers. The advantages of a 'cold press' juicer are threefold:

Better-quality juice
Better motor that lasts
Dry pulp so you save money on produce

The main movers in this field are juicers like the Green Star and Matstone, to name just a couple. The Green Star produces an extremely smooth and nutritious juice, but is really expensive and, like many slow juicers, a complete nightmare to clean. However, there are new upright slow juicers like the Hurom and Oscar 930, and these are slightly cheaper and produce a wonderful juice. At the time of writing, the **Retro Cold Press** upright juicer is the new, slick juicing kid on the block and seems to be stealing all the headlines. Not only because it produces a great juice, leaves dry pulp and you can put a whole apple in, but it is simply the coolest juicer on the market (go to **www.retrojuicer.com** and you'll see what I mean). However, the slow juicer market is ever-changing so, to see what's hot in the cold press juicer market right now, jump to **www.juicemaster.com**.

Low-induction Juicers

These are the 'halfway house' between slow and fast juicers. The 'godfather of fitness' and 'juicing guru' Jack LaLanne was one of the first to bring out a juicer of this nature. It was named after him and the Jack LaLanne Power Juicer went on to become the bestselling juicer in the US for over a decade. Sadly Jack passed away at the age of 96 and I was asked to try and fill his incredible boots. They changed the juicer slightly, but it was still a 'low-induction' juicer and they renamed it Jason Vale's Fusion Juicer. This type of juicer juices at speeds of about 3,000 rpm, so much slower than a 'fast' juicer but not as slow as a 'cold press' or 'slow' juicer – it's the middle ground, so to speak. However, what I soon discovered was that if someone was accustomed to using a fast juicer and then switched to a Fusion, they were often left disappointed. As my name was written all over the juicer, it was me who personally got the abuse from those who thought the juicer was a pile of crap and not working properly. The only reason they thought this was because they were comparing it to their previous fast juicer, a completely different kind of machine. It would be like comparing a Fiat 500 and a Mini Cooper S: both get you from A to B but each has different engines and their own unique upside. It's whether or not that upside is also *your* upside. If you like being economical, then the Fiat is for you; if you want speed, then it's the Mini Cooper. The truth is, the Fusion Juicer's low-induction motor is slower to use and takes a little getting used to, but it does indeed produce a superior juice. It was also much cheaper, in many cases, than the fast juicer. I thought this ticked all the boxes and was happy to put my name to it – you got better quality juice than a fast juicer, it was quicker to use than a slow juicer and it was relatively cheap. What I didn't account for was the fact that, because it looked like a fast juicer, people wanted it to perform exactly like a fast juicer and, when comparing the two machines, it seems speed was what they wanted over anything else. Contrary to what people think, I never owned the Fusion Juicer; I simply put my name to it and got very, very little in return (again contrary to popular belief). The reason I did put my name to it was that I was incredibly honoured to be asked by the big Americans to take over from the incredible Jack LaLanne and I honestly thought the juicer was the best of all worlds. I still think the Fusion Juicer fills that gap, but it appears it's a gap most don't want or understand. I have removed my name from this juicer and, as far as I know, it's now been discontinued. You can still buy them here and there and I still stand by the fact that, for the money, they produce one hell of an amazing-quality juice. I guess it's like the Betamax and VHS (yes, I am showing my age here) battle for the video tape years ago. Despite the Sony Betamax tape being far superior, better quality and smaller, the chunky VHS won and Betamax went into rapid decline, never to be heard of again. We may see low-induction juicing again, but perhaps with such wonderful fast and cold press juicers, people want either one or the other – not the in-betweener that seemed, on the surface, to be the answer. Like the Betamax before it, perhaps the Fusion Juicer may be assigned to the history books.

This is why I now say the best juicer to get is the one you will use! So pick a juicer that's right for *you* and *your* needs, not necessarily what's new on the market. Having said that, if this 'one-click, semi-self-cleaning' juicer becomes a reality, I'll be 'clicking to basket' quicker than you can say, 'Juice me up, baby!'

BUT WHAT JUICER DO YOU USE, JASON?

Over the years I have personally used many, many different juicers, but the one I have come back to time and time again, is the Philips 1861. Unfortunately, despite me wanting to buy the rights from Philips for this machine, Philips decided to discontinue it. They then reinvented the juicer with an upside-down bowl so you could see the juice being made and the pulp was hidden. Great idea on the surface, but if you are juicing for a few people, the juicer gets clogged as there's no separate pulp container. I will never, ever understand why Philips stopped making the 1861 as every juicer they have brought out since, in my opinion, just isn't as good. Now, before you jump on eBay looking for one of these, the good news is that something has come along to take its place and I now use this one a lot of the time – the **Retro Super Fast Juicer**. I also use the **Retro Cold Press** when I have more time. I am a firm believer that if you are only going to have one juice a day, do it right. That means organic where possible and made in a slow juicer. This isn't always convenient and at times speed is everything, which is why I use different machines depending on the time I have available. I also use the Fusion here and there to mix it up! I will point out that the reason I am such a fan of Retro at the moment is because they are, as I have mentioned, the coolest juicing kids on the block *and* they are great juicers. I'm an aesthetic person and they just look great in the kitchen. My mission is for people to *use* their juicer, not just buy one, and you're much more likely to leave it out on the work surface, primed and ready for use, if it looks good – and, boy, these look GOOD! I also have a **Retro Super Blend**; it's like a NutriBullet-type blender, only again it looks SO GOOD, and it matches my cold press and fast juicer. These are the juicers I use, but they may well not be the juicers for *your* needs. Do the research and find what *you* like and what fits with *your* kitchen.

WHICH BLENDER/SMOOTHIE MAKER?

A blender and a smoothie maker are one and the same thing. It was Kenwood who managed to get people who already owned a blender to go out and also buy a smoothie maker. So many people think they are somehow different, but in reality it is like calling a pan an 'egg boiler'!

There are many good blenders on the market these days but there are also some terrible models out there. When buying a blender you want to make sure it can blend ice and *frozen* fruits with speed and ease. One thing you don't want for this programme is a hand-blender – you need one with a plastic or glass jug.

To see my full recommendations, go to **www. juicemaster.com** or call the juicy team (0845 130 28 29).

WANT TO CONTINUE YOUR JUICY JOURNEY?

For free recipes, downloads, apps, more books and info about what juicer to get and what's on offer log onto:

www.juicemaster.com

If you want to get all the fruit and vegetables you need for the programme sent direct to your door with one click of the button, go to:

www.juicemasterfreshbox.com

Feeling lazy? If you want us to make all the juices for you and send them to you ready-made nip over to:

www.juicemasterdelivered.com

Fancy full juice and exercise immersion at a stunning health retreat? Log onto:

www.juicyoasis.com

www.juicymountain.com

Follow us on Twitter: **@juicemaster**

Or find us on Facebook: **Facebook.com/juicemasterltd**

Or on Google+: **plus.google.com/+juicemaster**

Or on Juice Tube!: **www.youtube.com/user/juicemasterjasonvale**

Or on Instagram: **@jasonvale**